SMOKIN' IN THE BOYS' ROOM

SMOKIN' IN THE BOYS' ROOM

Southern Recipes from the Winningest Woman in Barbecue

Melissa Cookston

Photography by
Angie Mosier

Andrews McMeel
Publishing, LLC

Kansas City • Sydney • London

Andrews McMeel Publishing, LLC
an Andrews McMeel Universal company
1130 Walnut Street, Kansas City, Missouri 64106

www.andrewsmcmeel.com
www.yazoosdeltaq.com

14 15 16 17 18 SHO 10 9 8 7 6 5 4 3 2 1

ISBN: 978-1-4494-4198-2

Library of Congress Control Number: 2013915649

Photography and styling by Angie Mosier
Photo pages xi, 61, 64, 72, 92, 105, 106, 113, 121, 123, 144,
    155, 156 © iStockphoto
Design by Holly Ogden

ATTENTION: SCHOOLS AND BUSINESSES
Andrews McMeel books are available at quantity discounts with bulk purchase for educational, business, or sales promotional use. For information, please e-mail the Andrews McMeel Publishing Special Sales Department: specialsales@amuniversal.com

CONTENTS

INTRODUCTION

MY STORY

Smokin' in the Boys' Room grew out of my seventeen years of cooking on the male-dominated barbecue contest circuit. Going back even further, it's also the natural product of a childhood spent around pit-fired barbecue, combined with an innate ultra-competitive spirit. Traditionally, the home kitchen has been women's domain, while the grill has been male territory. Maybe it's the caveman effect—big pieces of meat and fire bringing out the chest-thumping. That didn't stop me from reveling in my Mississippi Delta upbringing, where eating pulled-pork sandwiches while talking with my grandfather for hours on end as a child gave me a love for good southern barbecue.

I have always wanted to win, no matter the game or the stakes involved. I'm too old to play basketball, and I don't bowl, so entering barbecue contests was a great release for me. In my career as a pitmaster, I have been very happy just to make something I'm proud of turning in to judges, but winning a big contest such as the Memphis in May World Championship Barbecue Cooking Contest still makes me happier than a tornado in a trailer park.

In fact, I am the winningest woman in barbecue, and frankly, it's not even close. I was thrilled to reign as the Memphis in May Grand Champion in 2010 and 2012. I won the Whole Hog category both of those years and also managed to win Whole Hog in 2011 but lost the Grand Championship by 1 point (out of a possible 570!). In 2012, I won the Kingsford Invitational, where eight winners of the biggest contests in the barbecue world were invited to compete in the first true barbecue contest of champions. Not only did I win the Grand, but I also won first place in four out of five categories. (Those fellas were pretty surprised when a "Memphis pork" cook won the brisket category!)

Generally speaking, most men (cooks or judges) on the circuit are very cordial and nice to me. However, I have run into a few over the years who think my husband, Pete, needs to stick me back in the house. The looks on their faces make winning that much sweeter.

I've been called the "Queen of Q" (among some other choice names—men don't like getting beaten), but I'd prefer to be known as the "best barbecue cook" instead of the "best woman cook." Even though I'm the winningest woman, very few men have the résumé I have. There are no women's tees on the barbecue contest circuit, and I don't get a head start because I'm a girl. At the end of the day, barbecue is the great equalizer. It doesn't matter whether you are a man or woman, rich or poor, black or white; good barbecue crosses all those lines.

As competitive as I am, I am very appreciative of and humbled by the awards and acclaim I've received, and I'm the first to admit I didn't do it all by myself. With Pete and my daughter, Lauren, our team has cooked at barbecue contests not just as a way to make a living but also as a family adventure. In 2010, for example, we were in Washington, D.C., cooking on Pennsylvania Avenue at the Safeway National Capital Barbecue Battle, and one week later, we were in California, cooking for the *BBQ Pitmasters* television show. Let me tell you—if you aren't pretty close to your family, a solid month of traveling and cooking will sure get you there!

I have always been in the restaurant business in one form or fashion. I had my first job at a local restaurant when I was thirteen years old and have remained in the food business ever since. In 2007,

my husband and I decided we were going to enter the barbecue competition circuit full time—talk about a feast-or-famine existence! Luckily, we were smiled upon by the barbecue gods and did very well. However, with a child, running up and down the road every week going to contests is not an ideal way to make a living, so we looked for what would be the next step from the contest world. In 2011, we opened the Memphis Barbecue Company in Horn Lake, Mississippi. I wanted the restaurant to focus on barbecue and food from the Delta, and we made sure everything was made from scratch. We have had lines out the door every day since day one. We were so well received that we have opened locations in other cities to help spread the gospel of Memphis-style barbecue.

Smokin' in the Boys' Room comes from my heart. Here you'll find recipes I used to win world barbecue championships, recipes from my restaurants, and recipes I use to cook dinner on a Tuesday night. They are all recipes from my soul and upbringing, and I hope you enjoy them.

MEMPHIS-STYLE BARBECUE AND FOODS FROM THE DELTA

We are all products of our childhood. That everyday meal you hated as a child is often the one that drives your cravings as an adult.

I grew up in the Delta region, an area spanning from Memphis to New Orleans along the mighty Mississippi River, and it truly shaped my thinking about cooking and recipes. I once watched an episode of *The Frugal Gourmet* as a child, back when we had only about four TV channels and no remote control. The host, Jeff Smith, kept talking about "peasant food"—dishes cooked by the poor using the ingredients that the upper class didn't want, dishes that achieved the sublime from the mundane. I didn't get it at the time and was pretty happy when someone changed the channel, but I remember that show because Smith's point has become more and more important to me as I have matured. And as I've matured, I've become ever more infatuated with the flavorful food of the Delta.

Barbecue in general, and Delta cooking specifically, are all descended from the same mentality—turning tough ribs into world-championship cuisine, cooking a picnic shoulder full of fat and gristle for fifteen hours until the meat is succulent and dripping with flavor, using cheap masa flour and a couple of pounds of pork

to make tamales that speak to you. Delta cuisine is not necessarily soul food, although it shares some dishes. It sure isn't Cajun or Creole, although I'd call it a second cousin once removed. It is food focused on fresh ingredients, and it is intensely flavored. It is a food made by people, white and black, poor and wealthy, who know that everyday (cheaper) ingredients and meats cooked properly can be just as satisfying as the meals reserved for Sunday. It's about food prepared with love, care, and passion.

Memphis-style barbecue has been such a defining influence in my life. When I was younger, I remember my mother getting a craving for ribs, bundling us up in the car, and driving two hours to a famous Memphis restaurant just to eat ribs. At the time, I thought it was absolutely crazy to drive hours each way just to eat ribs, but now I get it. One day, my mother, being a "can do" type of person, decided that she could do her own ribs just as well as that restaurant. She went to the meat market and purchased some beautiful ribs, got her seasonings together, and fired up the grill. The smell was heavenly—for a while. A few hours later, we were in the car heading to Memphis again, and "the great rib experiment" was never mentioned again. Memphis-style barbecue has that kind of effect on people.

Memphis barbecue is about meats cooked low and slow and seasoned with a soulful hand. It is about texture—pork butts and shoulders cooked to the exact moment where the meat can be pulled by hand into succulent pieces and never needs to be chopped. Ribs are cooked so the meat can come cleanly from the bone but still maintain integrity, body, and a wonderful mouthfeel. Cooking pork to those textures is really about flavor. Properly cooked pork allows the meat to express its own innate flavor, in addition to any seasonings and sauces, across your palate. Memphis barbecue has a full-flavored profile, with a sweet beginning note and a symphony of savory and spicy melodies that sing in your mouth the way B. B. King plays his guitar. The phrase "sweet with a little heat" pretty much sums up Memphis-style barbecue, and that well-rounded flavor profile is exactly what you'll find in my recipes.

Finally, Memphis barbecue and Delta cooking are also about using fresh, local products. When I was growing up, my grandparents always had a large garden. Not only would we get fresh cucumbers, cabbage, corn, and tomatoes at the very peak of freshness, they would also "put up" plenty of peas and butterbeans to get through the long winter. I never really developed a green thumb to grow my own garden, but I do love to go to farmers' markets to get the wonderful vegetables that I grew up enjoying. I am so glad to see the locavore movement grow. The large chain groceries have their place in everyday life, but it is so much more rewarding and enjoyable to me to be able to purchase heritage pork, locally grown produce, and farm-fresh milk, eggs, and other foods that I used to take for granted but now yearn to have. Whenever possible, I try to buy fresh and local. This "movement" in the culinary world of today is really just a revisiting of the everyday life of people before the advent of "factory farms" and long-haul trucking. Whether you're making my Smoked Tomato Bisque, Balsamic Grilled Vegetables, Corn Casserole, Blackberry Chutney, or Mississippi Caviar, fresh and local always taste better.

MISSISSIPPI
Providence
Monroe
Greenville
Columbus
Jackson
Vicksburg
Meridian
Natchez
Hattiesburg
Laurel
Tombigbee R.

PANTRY

1

THE BASICS

Every cook has a go-to list of pantry items. As a home cook and a contest cook, I typically keep two pantries, with a lot of ingredients stocked in both. Since we're focusing mostly on home cooking, the following represent what I consider must-haves for the home pantry and what you'll need to cook most of the recipes in this book. They'll still allow you to make succulent, championship-quality barbecue and give you a nice base for creating your own recipes.

Spices and Aromatics

★ Kosher, table, sea, and finishing salts. (I really have gotten addicted to some of these—they provide a wonderful texture without an overwhelming salt flavor.)
★ Black peppercorns and coarsely and finely ground black pepper
★ Granulated garlic and whole fresh garlic
★ Onion powder, dehydrated onions (dried onion flakes), and fresh onions (preferably Vidalia, if in season)
★ Whole cinnamon sticks
★ Coriander and cumin seeds
★ Dill seeds and celery seeds
★ Dried oregano, thyme, and basil
★ Dry mustard
★ Paprika
★ Light and dark chili powder
★ Ancho chile powder
★ Chipotle chile powder
★ Cayenne
★ Hot red pepper flakes

Oils, Vinegars, and Other Acids

★ Good-quality extra virgin olive oil
★ Canola oil
★ Balsamic vinegar (a very good one for dressings and one more suited for marinades and reductions)

- ★ Red wine vinegar
- ★ White vinegar
- ★ Cider vinegar
- ★ Lemon juice (bottled is fine)
- ★ Unsweetened lime juice (bottled is fine)

Sweeteners
- ★ Turbinado sugar (a must-have for my barbecue recipes)
- ★ Granulated (white) sugar
- ★ Blackstrap molasses
- ★ Light and dark brown sugar
- ★ Honey (preferably local, single source)
- ★ Agave syrup

Other Ingredients
- ★ Canned tomatoes (preferably San Marzano)
- ★ Yellow and white self-rising cornmeal
- ★ Baking powder and baking soda
- ★ Self-rising and all-purpose flours
- ★ Canned tomato sauce
- ★ Tomato paste
- ★ Evaporated milk
- ★ Sweetened condensed milk
- ★ Good-quality ketchup
- ★ Worcestershire sauce
- ★ Whole chipotles in adobo sauce
- ★ Yellow mustard
- ★ Hot sauce
- ★ Sugar cure (available online)
- ★ Chicken, beef, and bacon bases. (I prefer pastes, preferably Minor's brand.)

TIP

In general, I purchase my spices whole, if possible, and grind them myself. I keep a spare coffee grinder around just for this purpose. Spices lose their potency quickly, so try to keep them as fresh as possible. In addition to a good selection of dried staples, I try to keep several fresh herbs in the fridge. To keep them longer, store them stem down in a small cup of water in the fridge. ★

BASIC, MUST-HAVE TOOLS

Mortar and Pestle ★ This tool is useful for mixing small amounts of pastes, slathers, and sauces, and it travels well without needing electricity.

Knives ★ Invest in a good set of knives and you will have them for years. My favorite knife series is Mac Knives (macknife.com). These combine the sharpness and durability of a Japanese blade with the extra heft of a European-style knife. These are really good knives. For my contest set, I have a 12-inch slicer with a dimpled edge (small indentions in the side of the knife to make it easier to slide through a product), 8-inch santoku (really my favorite knife ever—I don't know how I got along without it before!), two 6-inch utility knives, and two 6-inch curved boning knives.

Charcoal Chimney ★ A chimney helps you get your charcoal going without lighter fluid, which can give your final

product a chemical taste. Just place an electric charcoal starter in it, fill it with briquettes, set it on a heatproof surface or in the bottom of your grill, and wait until the briquettes look ashy (about 20 minutes) before dumping them into the cooker. If you don't have an electric starter, you can put a few wads of paper or newsprint underneath and light the paper with a match or lighter.

Electric Charcoal Starter ★ A starter is easier to use than matches/paper to light your chimney, especially on a windy day.

"Hot Gloves" ★ This is what I call cotton gloves that are thin enough that you can put nitrile gloves on over them. They make a huge difference when pulling hot meat.

Pastry Brushes ★ My go-to brush for sauce is a 2-inch synthetic-bristle brush, which leaves the fewest brush strokes when glazing or saucing meats.

Tongs and Metal Pizza Peels ★ It's easy to burn yourself when you move food around on the grill. I keep some quality (strong) 12-inch tongs for moving ribs and to use while grilling, as well as some shorter (6-inch) tongs for more delicate maneuvers. A pizza peel is great for larger cuts of meat, such as butts or shoulders.

TOOLS I'D RATHER NOT DO WITHOUT

I am a firm believer in knowing the basics of barbecue cooking without fancy tools and gadgets. If you give me an old barrel grill with no thermometer, a few spices, some meat, and really nothing else, I'm confident that I will be able to produce a pretty tasty product that's fairly close to competition quality. However, since we live in an age when some pretty smart folks make all these cool toys for cooking, why not use them?

Meat Maximizer 45-Blade Meat Tenderizer ★ Made by Jaccard (and often called by that name), this is a spring-loaded contraption with forty-five very small knives that you press across meats to tenderize them. This is a great way to tenderize without mashing your steak, especially when cooking sirloins, strip steaks, pork chops, or flank steak.

Meat Injectors ★ I keep quite a few small needle injectors around, as well as a larger, pump-type injector. The larger injector is indispensable for multiple shoulders or hogs, but it too big for delicate cuts of meat. I don't inject as much liquid as some of my competitors do, so I avoid the brine pumps.

Meat Thermometers ★ I am always willing to spend money to have the best thermometers I can find. Always make sure they are calibrated by checking the temperature of boiling water (212°F at sea level)—even the good ones get bumped out of temp at times. Most decent thermometers have dials that you can use to adjust the gauge to bring it back to the right reading. I always have meat thermometers that I can leave in meat while it's cooking, as well as instant-read thermometers to test the meat. That being said, there is no better way to test tenderness than learning how to use your fingers. We cooked contests for many years without even a stick thermometer around—it was all about time, temperature, and texture and learning to check things by feel, typically by poking the meat with an index finger. Basically, you are simply trying to determine the doneness of the meat by checking the texture. There is really no way to teach you by telling you what something should feel like when it's done perfectly. Simply practice every time you cook, taking note of how meat feels at various stages of doneness. If it feels moist and tender, it probably is!

Immersion Blender or Stick Blender ★ These are invaluable for mixing injections or sauces, emulsifying dressings, or pureeing soup.

Controlled Draft Systems ★ Many contest cooks use these to help control the temperature of their pits. Basically, these are fan-driven thermostats for smokers. I never have 100 percent faith in these tools, but they can make it possible for you to walk away from your cooker for an hour or so.

Insulated Coolers or Cambros ★ In the restaurant business, we use large insulated boxes (often called "Cambros" after the leading manufacturer) for transporting food to catering sites. Most of these have built-in slots for sliding in aluminum pans, which make them very convenient. They work great for the contest barbecue cook, too, as you may have multiple meats you need to hold or rest. You can just as easily use a regular cooler instead, especially for home use.

Electric Reciprocating Saw ★ If I had to pick my favorite thing to do in the barbecue world, it would be to start trimming a hog with a big, dangerous-looking saw—immensely satisfying.

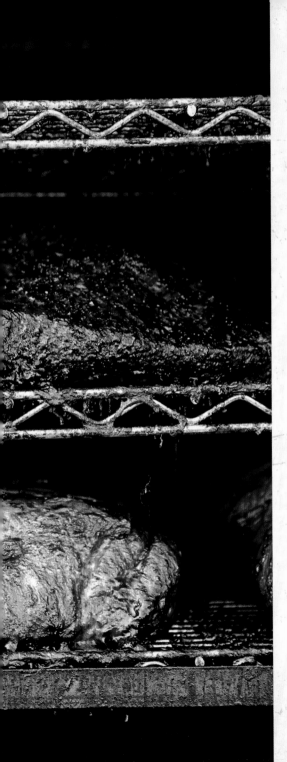

You'll need this only for very large cuts of meat or getting through a lot of bone. A regular electric meat-cutting knife also comes in handy for general use.

SMOKERS

I learned to cook on old-fashioned barrel grills with no thermometers. I've burned down wood into charcoal and had to learn how to feed concrete pits to avoid hot spots and flame-ups. I've slept many a cold night underneath the hot box of a barrel grill, and when I finally made the move to insulated cookers, I was both relieved and saddened. (I managed to adapt to the modern world pretty quickly, and now I get a few cat naps in at night!) These insulated water cookers allow me to concentrate on my product rather than fighting the cooker. However, there are many other types of smokers that people use with great success—from custom smokers that cost thousands of dollars to a basic kettle-style grill. The main thing is to learn your own pit and then adapt your cooking times.

I am not a purist who believes only charcoal and wood can make true barbecue or grilled items. Yes, I think you get better flavor, but I've eaten many delicious items prepared on a gas grill, especially when used with a smoker box attachment.

CHARCOAL AND WOODS

A lot of people think that all barbecue is about is how much smoke flavor you can put on a piece of meat. If you go around and taste barbecue champions' products all over the country, however, you will notice that while smoke is an integral component of their flavor profile, it is subtle and works with the other aspects of their flavors. The lesson here is simple: Use smoke in moderation, just as you would with any other ingredient. It should complement, not overwhelm.

When using most smokers, it is most effective to keep a base fire of charcoal and use wood chunks to add smoke and flavor. Every smoker is different, and the amount of wood you need to use will vary by brands or types. I may use four to six chunks of wood on a charcoal fire. This will typically be enough for three hours of smoking. Another aspect that really impacts your flavor is having a "clean" fire. Make sure your pit has proper air intake and exhaust, or you may get a sooty taste or an overly dark product.

There are many types of wood available, and I've tried quite a few, but I mainly use cherry, apple, peach, pecan, and hickory, or some combination of those, depending on the meat. I'd say I use cherry for contests 80 percent of the time, because it yields a beautiful smoke ring that will help your appearance scores in a contest setting.

Cherry ★ A full, robust flavor with a beautiful, bright red smoke ring

Apple ★ Sweet, light flavor and light pink smoke ring

Peach ★ Gives results somewhere between apple and cherry and smells absolutely great while burning

Pecan ★ Beautiful smoke ring with golden accents and a neutral smoke flavor

Hickory ★ Best used as an accent wood, as it can turn your product dark and bitter if used too much. (I typically throw in one or two chunks at the beginning of a cook to "set" my smoke flavor. This means it allows me to get a smoke flavor without the overwhelming taste of hickory.)

VERY
SUPERSTITIOUS

Let me tell you—barbecue folks are some superstitious people, myself included. For years, whenever we won a contest, we had to keep some item from the contest site with us. At one time, we were toting around a matchbox car, a brick, a wooden pole, several scrap pieces of metal, a faded dollar bill, and a 36-inch saw blade. On a trip to Louisiana one year, we had an actual voodoo lady put some good luck on our smokers and our special "totem." After word of our totem leaked out, other teams would surreptitiously try to rub the charm. This resulted in us having to keep it locked up at contests—no stealing of the mojo allowed!

When we were cooking contests every week (and when whether we got to eat the next week depended on winning), we were about as superstitious as you can get. We had certain clothes we wore on certain days (including underwear!), certain songs we would play, certain sayings we would use, etc. You have to work hard if you want to keep the good juju around! ★

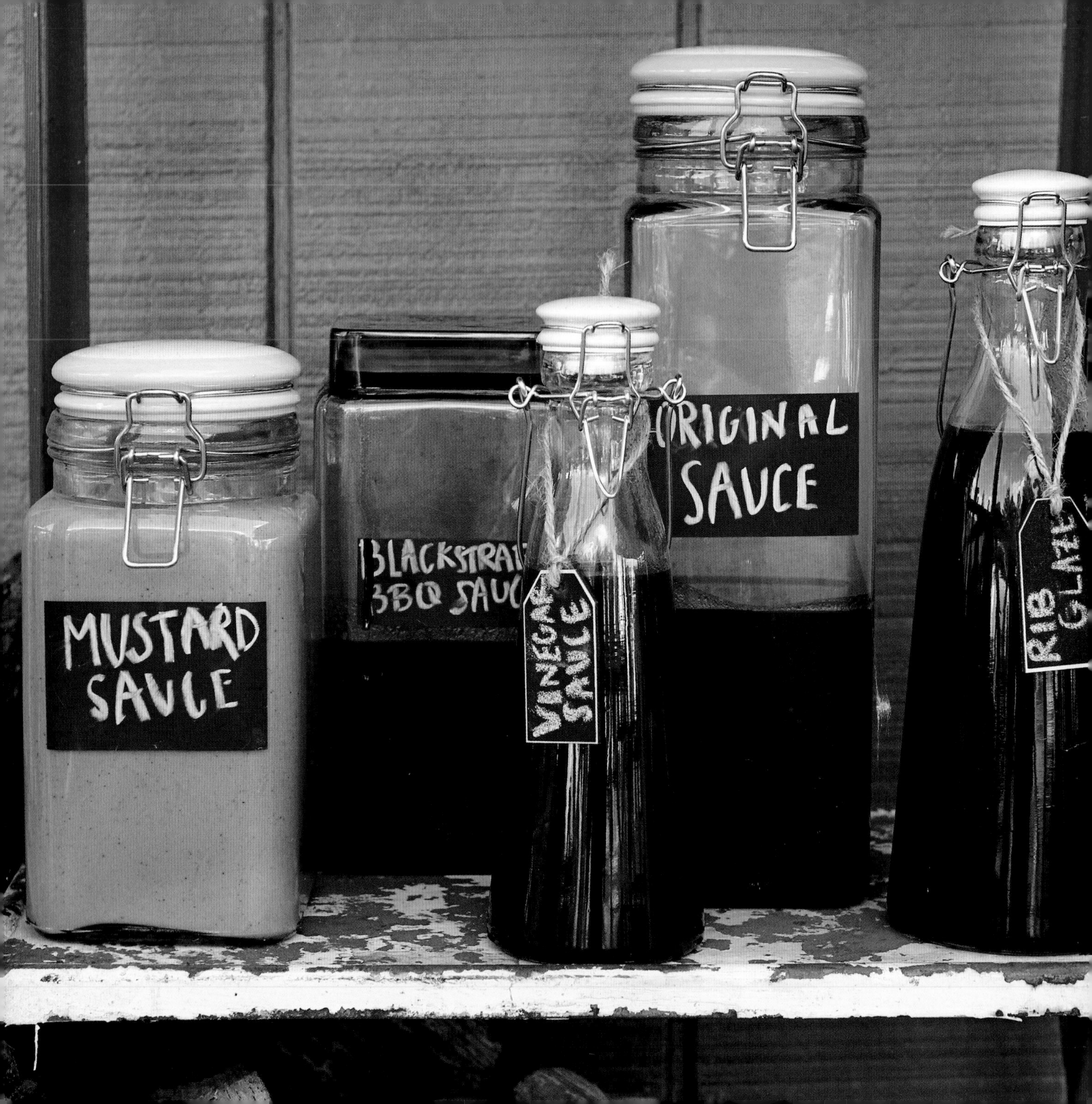
MUSTARD SAUCE
VINEGAR SAUCE
ORIGINAL SAUCE
RIB

My barbecue and cooking are about building layered tastes that unite on the palate to create a wonderful full-flavored effect. Seasoning blends, more commonly known in the barbecue world as *rubs,* are the main flavoring agents for barbecuing meats and form the cornerstone of my recipes. We use our rubs as the glue that binds the meat to the sauce, and by using them as an integral component in the injections as well, I achieve a complementary taste effect for my meats.

I am very picky about selecting spices as well as keeping them fresh. With time and exposure to air, spices lose their potency, so it is paramount that you keep them in a sealed container and use them within a few months. I prefer to purchase spices whole and grind them myself using a grinder or mortar and pestle. However, for the recipes in the book, I have listed the ground amounts needed.

I use injections in competitions to maximize moisture and add a base layer of flavor. My injections are an internal brine, rather than merely a method of flavoring. My pork stock and beef stock recipes serve as the foundation of the injections. Generally speaking, I am a big advocate of scratch cooking, and I make my own stocks. However, I have also used concentrated pastes in a ratio of ¼ cup of paste to 1 gallon of water for competition injections with very good results. (It has to be concentrated.) The drawback to using pastes is the sodium level. If you use prepared pastes, I recommend Minor's brand, as they are high quality and not as salty as others. An injection that's too salty will overwhelm the final taste of the meat. Taste before using!

Sauces are the final layer of flavoring I add to meat. Ensuring a wonderful marriage between meat and sauce is the key to a great product, whether in a contest or at home.

2
SEASONINGS, INJECTIONS, AND SAUCES

Sauce should complement the meat, not overpower it, and certainly never conflict with it. This is why I have purposely developed my competition sauces to include our competition rubs. In my world, there are two distinct types of sauce—competition and "any other." I've included some of both. My competition sauces have sweet accents but a well-rounded flavor. I tell every judge to put a little sauce on his or her finger, then on the front of the tongue. The flavor should travel all across the palate—a little sweet, a little acid, a little salt, and a kick at the back to tell you it was there!

With my "other" sauces, I'm not as worried about the exact right notes for a judge's palate, and I can accent certain flavors that I want to use to bring out the best qualities in the dish. As an example, my Blackstrap BBQ Sauce recipe highlights blackstrap molasses, one of my favorite flavors from growing up in the Delta.

During a contest week, I make my barbecue rubs on Tuesdays and competition sauces and injections on Wednesdays for the weekend event. When tasting your seasoning blends and sauces, it is easy to get "palate fatigue" to the point where you miss how something would taste to a judge, so I always try to spread out the tasks to ensure I can taste the flavors properly. Making your sauces a few days before the contest also gives you a better opportunity to redo them if you make a mistake or discover you are missing a key ingredient. It also allows you to concentrate on trimming meat, packing for the contest, and traveling later in the week. Contests are tough, so if you plan to participate in them, have a plan and work it in order to make it go much more smoothly!

BASIC BBQ RUB

Makes about 2¾ cups

This is my basic rub when I'm cooking at home. It also serves as the base rub for my Ultimate BBQ Rub, which follows, a fired-up version for the competition circuit. The difference is between eating half a slab of ribs at the house or a couple of bites on the competition trail. When you want to make a meal of something, you may not want it as potent.

1 cup turbinado sugar

½ cup granulated sugar

½ cup kosher salt

1 tablespoon onion powder

2 tablespoons granulated garlic

1½ teaspoons cayenne

1 teaspoon finely ground black pepper

2 teaspoons dry mustard

¼ cup light chili powder

1 teaspoon ground cumin (see Note, page 16)

¼ cup plus 2 tablespoons paprika

Place the turbinado sugar in a coffee grinder and pulse until lightly powdered. Transfer to a small mixing bowl and add the granulated sugar, salt, onion powder, granulated garlic, cayenne, black pepper, dry mustard, chili powder, cumin, and paprika. Stir until well incorporated. Store in an airtight container for up to 1 month.

ULTIMATE BBQ RUB

Makes about 6½ cups

In competitions, a judge may take as little as one bite of your product—so you have to amp up the flavors. The judges tend to like flavors with more punch on both ends of the palate (both the sweet and spicy areas), so this version kicks up the flavor components a few notches.

1 cup turbinado sugar
5 cups Basic BBQ Rub (page 13)
¼ cup light chili powder
¼ cup granulated garlic
1 teaspoon cayenne

Place the turbinado sugar in a clean coffee grinder and pulse until lightly powdered. Transfer to a large mixing bowl. (You may have to work in batches.) Add the rub, chili powder, granulated garlic, and cayenne and stir until well incorporated. Store in an airtight container for up to 2 months.

DELTA CREOLE SEASONING

Makes about ¾ cup

I use this whenever I want a little more kick in a sauce or whenever I'm bronzing chicken, fish, or pork. It also works great as a barbecue rub for smoked pork tenderloin.

2 tablespoons paprika

3 tablespoons kosher salt

2 tablespoons granulated garlic

1 tablespoon coarsely ground
   black pepper

1 tablespoon onion powder

1 teaspoon cayenne, or to taste

1 tablespoon dried oregano

1 teaspoon dried basil

1 tablespoon dried thyme

Combine all the ingredients in a small mixing bowl and stir by hand until well incorporated. Store in an airtight container for up to 1 month.

FAJITA SEASONING

Makes about 1 cup

I used to buy a fajita seasoning in the grocery store that I really liked, and I used it for many more things than fajitas. One day, I couldn't find it anymore, so I made my own version. I use this on many things when cooking at the house. It doesn't really have a typical Mexican food flavor, but rather just a well-rounded spice blend that livens up everything from meats to vegetables.

½ cup kosher salt

¼ cup granulated garlic

2 tablespoons coarsely ground black pepper

½ teaspoon light chili powder

½ teaspoon chipotle chile powder

1 teaspoon ground cumin (see Note)

1 teaspoon onion powder

Place all the ingredients in a small mixing bowl and stir until well incorporated. Store in an airtight container for up to 2 months.

NOTE

Right before mixing any seasoning blends containing cumin, I like to lightly toast the cumin in a clean, dry skillet over medium heat for about 2 minutes or until aromatic. This brings out the oils and really improves the flavor.

GRILL SEASONING

Makes about 1¾ cups

This is my all-purpose grilling seasoning, as I like the saltier overtones for the grill. It's great on steaks, pork chops, and grilled chicken.

½ cup freshly cracked black pepper

1 tablespoon dried onion flakes

1 tablespoon coriander seeds

1 tablespoon dill seeds

1 teaspoon hot red pepper flakes

1 cup kosher salt

2 tablespoons granulated garlic

1 teaspoon light chili powder

1 teaspoon ground cumin (see Note)

Place the cracked black pepper, onion flakes, coriander seeds, dill seeds, and hot red pepper flakes in a coffee grinder and pulse until reduced in size but not pulverized. Transfer to a small mixing bowl, add the salt, granulated garlic, chili powder, and cumin, and stir until well incorporated. Store in an airtight container for up to 1 month.

PORK COMPETITION INJECTION

Makes enough for 6 shoulders or 1 medium whole hog

Competition barbecue is a challenge. On one hand, you must have a rich, bold flavor, but on the other hand you can't overwhelm the natural flavors of the meat. My pork injection amplifies the natural pork flavors and helps integrate them with my seasonings and sauces.

1 gallon Pork Stock (recipe follows)

1 cup Ultimate BBQ Rub (page 14)

1 cup apple juice

1 cup Worcestershire sauce

1 cup light corn syrup, such as Karo

In a large stockpot, heat the pork stock to a brisk simmer. Whisk in the rub until thoroughly dissolved. Whisk in the apple juice, Worcestershire, and corn syrup and turn off the heat. Cool and store in an airtight container in the refrigerator for up to 5 days.

PORK STOCK

Makes 6 quarts

1 tablespoon canola oil

5 to 6 pounds pork rib trimmings (meat and bones)

2 cups coarsely chopped onion

1 cup coarsely chopped carrot

1 cup coarsely chopped celery

3 cloves garlic, minced

2 teaspoons salt

3 bay leaves

2 teaspoons freshly ground black pepper

8 quarts water

In a large stockpot, heat the oil over medium heat. Add the pork trimmings and cook for 20 minutes, stirring occasionally. Add the onion, carrot, celery, garlic, salt, bay leaves, and pepper and cook for 10 minutes. Add the water, bring to a boil, then decrease the heat and simmer, uncovered, for 3 to 4 hours, until reduced by half. Strain through a fine-mesh strainer. Cool and store in an airtight container in the refrigerator for up to 5 days.

BEEF COMPETITION INJECTION

Makes 2 quarts

I have the same philosophy about beef injections as I do with pork: I use them to amplify the natural flavors of the meat, not overwhelm them. This makes a rich, beefy injection that really helps a brisket over the long cooking process.

2 quarts Beef Stock (recipe
   follows)
½ cup Worcestershire sauce
⅓ cup Ultimate BBQ Rub
   (page 14)
2 tablespoons granulated garlic
2 teaspoons onion powder

In a large stockpot, heat the beef stock to a brisk simmer. Whisk in the Worcestershire, rub, granulated garlic, and onion powder until thoroughly incorporated and turn off the heat. This should taste like a very good, beefy jus. Cool and store in an airtight container in the refrigerator for up to 5 days.

BEEF STOCK

Makes 4 quarts

1 tablespoon canola oil
4 to 5 pounds beef trimmings
   (meat and bones)
2 cups coarsely chopped onion
1 cup coarsely chopped celery
1 cup coarsely chopped carrot
1 tablespoon black peppercorns
2 fresh thyme sprigs or 1
   teaspoon dried
3 bay leaves
6 quarts water

In a large stockpot, heat the oil over medium heat. Add the beef trimmings and cook for 20 minutes, stirring occasionally. Add the onion, celery, carrot, peppercorns, thyme, and bay leaves and cook for 10 minutes. Add the water and scrape the bottom of the pan with a spoon. Bring to a boil, then decrease the heat and simmer for 3 to 4 hours, until reduced by half. Strain through a fine-mesh strainer. Cool and store in an airtight container in the refrigerator for up to 5 days.

BBQ MOTHER SAUCE

Makes about 6 cups

This recipe has always been our "mother" competition sauce—the base we use to make the sauces we serve for competition judges. It is very forgiving of tweaking, so use it as a palette with which to add your favorite flavors. One of my favorite variations is to add a cup of peach or mango puree to 2 cups of the sauce for a fresh taste. When cooking competition chicken, I leave out the diced onion and substitute 1 tablespoon of onion powder, as I like a smoother finish on chicken.

¼ cup canola oil

¾ cup finely diced sweet or yellow onion

2 tablespoons minced garlic

1½ cups ketchup

½ cup honey

2 tablespoons tomato paste

¼ cup white vinegar

¼ cup plus 2 tablespoons packed dark brown sugar

¼ cup Worcestershire sauce

2 teaspoons dry mustard

1 teaspoon cayenne

1 teaspoon freshly ground black pepper

½ cup water, or as needed

½ cup Basic BBQ Rub (page 13) or Ultimate BBQ Rub (page 14), or to taste

In a medium saucepan, heat the oil over medium heat. Add the onion and sauté until translucent, about 5 minutes. Turn the heat to low if the onion is cooking too fast—you don't want it caramelized or browned. As the onion is getting close, add the garlic and cook until lightly golden, about 2 minutes longer. Add the ketchup, honey, tomato paste, vinegar, brown sugar, Worcestershire, dry mustard, cayenne, and black pepper and stir well. Slowly add water until the sauce reaches the consistency you like. A slightly thick consistency is best. Add about 3 tablespoons of the rub, stir well, and taste. The sauce should have a good, well-rounded flavor. Add more rub in 1-tablespoon increments until your desired flavor is achieved. Cool and store in an airtight container in the refrigerator for up to 10 days.

SWEET GLAZE

Makes 3 cups

Barbecue competitions are not just about flavor—they're also about appearance. Honey will not only add some sweetness but also give your products a beautiful sheen.

**2 cups BBQ Mother Sauce
(page 20)**

1 cup honey

**2 tablespoons Basic BBQ Rub
(page 13)**

In a small saucepan over low heat, stir the mother sauce with the honey until incorporated. Add the rub and stir until the sugars in the rub have dissolved and there is no grainy texture. Remove from the heat, cool, and store in an airtight container in the refrigerator for up to 2 weeks.

To use, brush on the meat in the last 10 minutes of smoking or 2 minutes of grilling (so the glaze doesn't burn).

CHIPOTLE BOLD BBQ SAUCE

Makes 3½ cups

This is my favorite sauce. I don't really think of it as a hot sauce, but the chipotle chiles add a wonderfully warm, smoky layer with a little bit of heat on the back end. If you like it hotter, just add more of the chipotle chile puree.

2 tablespoons white vinegar

1 (8-ounce can) chipotle chiles in adobo sauce

3 cups BBQ Mother Sauce (page 20)

1 tablespoon Ultimate BBQ Rub (page 14)

Puree the vinegar and chipotles together in a blender.

In a small stockpot over low heat, combine the mother sauce and rub. Heat until the sauce is warm, then add 2 tablespoons of the chipotle-vinegar puree. Stir and then taste. This is the heat level we serve for judges, but if you want it hotter, add 1 or 2 more tablespoons of the chipotle-vinegar puree. Cool and store in an airtight container in the refrigerator for up to 2 weeks. The sauce will get hotter as it sits, so be careful!

MEMPHIS-STYLE VINEGAR SAUCE

Makes 2¾ cups

This sauce won the 2012 Memphis in May World Championship for Vinegar Sauces. Honestly, I don't like most vinegar sauces I've tried. This sauce brings in some of the vinegar flavor but still has enough of a tomato base to keep it familiar to a Mississippi girl. I love serving this as a table sauce for whole hog or as a light glaze for meats like pork tenderloin or chicken.

2 cups BBQ Mother Sauce
  (page 20)
½ cup cider vinegar
2 tablespoons red wine vinegar
1 teaspoon hot red pepper flakes
1 teaspoon coarsely ground black
  pepper

In a small mixing bowl, whisk all the ingredients together until incorporated. Store in an airtight container in the refrigerator for up to 2 weeks.

BBQ BACON SAUCE

Makes 6 cups

This sauce is redolent with the smokiness of the bacon, which adds a nice texture as well. Use this blast of bacon flavor on a grilled pork chop or substitute it for ketchup in a meat loaf for an added boost of flavor.

1 pound Makin' Bacon (page 66) or your favorite brand, finely diced

½ cup minced yellow onion

1 tablespoon minced garlic

1 cup cider vinegar

½ cup ketchup

2 tablespoons tomato paste

2 tablespoons Worcestershire sauce

¼ cup honey

1 cup packed light brown sugar

2 teaspoons Ultimate BBQ Rub (page 14)

1 teaspoon cayenne

Place the bacon in a large stockpot over medium heat and cook until well rendered and crisp, about 5 minutes. Transfer the bacon to a paper-towel-lined plate and set aside. Drain off all but about 3 tablespoons of the grease from the stockpot. Add the onion and garlic to the pot and cook until translucent, about 5 minutes. Add the vinegar, ketchup, tomato paste, and Worcestershire. Bring to a boil, then decrease the heat to a simmer. Add the bacon, honey, brown sugar, rub, and cayenne and stir until incorporated. Continue to simmer for 8 to 10 minutes, until the sugar is broken down and the sauce is slightly reduced. Cool and store in an airtight container in the refrigerator for up to a week.

MUSTARD BBQ SAUCE

Makes 5 cups

Although certainly not traditional to the Delta, mustard barbecue sauces are the quiet cousins of tomato and vinegar sauces and share as lengthy a history as their more well-known relatives. Lately I've been playing around with them quite a bit, and this is one of my favorite recipes. Try it on any pork cut for a nice change.

2 cups yellow mustard

1 cup cider vinegar

½ cup packed dark brown sugar

½ cup ketchup

½ cup agave syrup or honey

1 teaspoon coarsely ground black pepper

2 teaspoons kosher salt

2 teaspoons granulated garlic

1 teaspoon dried onion flakes

1 teaspoon cayenne

In a small saucepan over medium heat, stir the mustard and vinegar together. Add the brown sugar, ketchup, agave syrup, black pepper, salt, granulated garlic, dried onion flakes, and cayenne and whisk until mixed thoroughly. Continue to heat until the sugar is dissolved fully. Cool and store in an airtight container in the refrigerator for up to 2 weeks.

BLACKSTRAP BBQ SAUCE

Makes 5 cups

Molasses is a way of life in the Delta. Every town used to have a farmer who would mill sugarcane using a mule-powered mill, then cook down the juice into cane syrup (the first boil), molasses (the second boil), or its most flavorful version from the final boil—blackstrap molasses. This thick, dark product can be a bit of an acquired taste but really adds richness to this sauce.

1½ teaspoons canola oil

2 tablespoons minced yellow
  onion

1 cup blackstrap molasses

1 cup ketchup

1 cup tomato sauce

½ cup cider vinegar

¼ cup Worcestershire sauce

2 teaspoons dry mustard

1 teaspoon paprika

1 teaspoon light chili powder

1½ teaspoons kosher salt

1 teaspoon granulated garlic

½ teaspoon coarsely ground
  black pepper

Heat the oil in a large saucepan over medium heat. Add the onion and cook until translucent, about 5 minutes. Add the molasses, ketchup, tomato sauce, vinegar, Worcestershire, dry mustard, paprika, chili powder, salt, granulated garlic, and pepper and bring to a boil, stirring occasionally. Decrease the heat and simmer for 20 to 30 minutes. Cool and store in an airtight container in the refrigerator for up to 2 weeks.

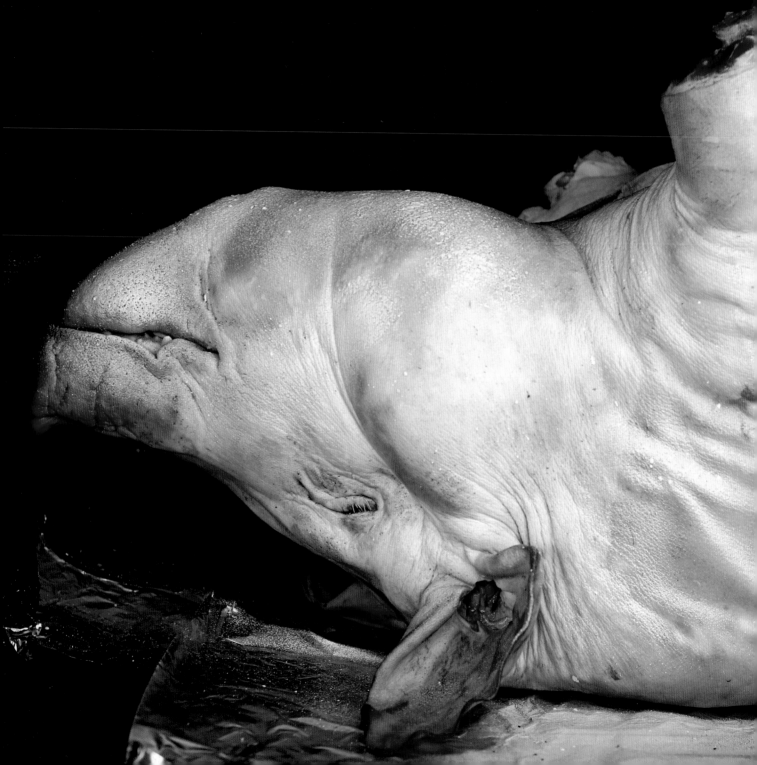

When you're from the Delta, pork is king, and you learn how to cook it or you go hungry a lot. The Delta's barbecue roots really show up in Memphis-style contests, which feature only pork—whole hog, ribs, or whole shoulders.

A lot of people seem to think *Memphis style* means dry ribs (ribs without a wet sauce applied). While these are available in the area restaurants, they are not predominately what people serve or order. I love a dry rib as much as the next person, but on a day-to-day basis wet ribs rule the roost. If you want to serve a dry rib, instead of saucing it at the end of cooking, just lightly sprinkle more dry rub on top and allow it to melt into the meat for a few minutes.

Memphis-style ribs are typically more tender than the ribs served in other areas, and generally speaking, baby back ribs are king. At a Memphis-style contest, 99 percent of the time teams will turn in baby backs.

In this chapter I have also included my lamb chop recipe. Yes, I am aware that lamb is not related to pork in lineage or in taste, but we did win a First Place at the World Championships with it, so I figured it might go pretty well in this chapter with so many winners from the pork category.

3

PORK AND LAMB

COMPETITION PORK BABY BACK RIBS

Serves 2 to 4, depending on whether they're linemen or cheerleaders

I'm known in the media and among competitors as a whole-hog cook, and I've been very fortunate with whole hogs in contests. However, I've won a lot more contests with my baby back ribs. This recipe won first place in eight contests in a row—a pretty mean feat! These ribs have a full flavor profile: a little sweet, some acid, a little salt, and just enough heat on the back of your palate to make you want another bite. Save the bones and meat trimmings for making stock (page 18).

2 slabs baby back ribs, about 3 pounds each (see Note, page 32)

¼ cup plus 2 tablespoons Ultimate BBQ Rub (page 14)

¼ cup plus 2 tablespoons yellow mustard

2 tablespoons honey

4 tablespoons turbinado sugar

4 tablespoons purple grape juice

About ½ cup Sweet Glaze (page 21)

Chipotle chile powder, for sprinkling

Rinse the ribs and remove the membrane from the back. Trim any excess fat from the tops of the slabs. Trim 1 bone from the large end of the ribs and 2 bones from the small end. This will give you a much more consistent slab for cooking.

Starting on the backs, sprinkle the ribs with approximately 1½ teaspoons of rub each, then add 1½ teaspoons mustard each and massage into the meat. Flip the ribs over and repeat. Wrap tightly in plastic wrap and refrigerate for at least 8 hours. For a contest, I marinate ribs like this for 12 to 16 hours.

Prepare a smoker to cook at 225°F with around 4 chunks of apple wood and 4 chunks of cherry wood so that the wood will smolder throughout the cooking. Remove the ribs from the refrigerator, unwrap, and repeat the rub and mustard procedure, massaging them in. Don't get it too thick or pastelike, as this will give you a dark appearance when cooked.

Place the ribs in the smoker meat side up and cook for 2 hours. Remove the ribs from the smoker and increase the temperature to 250°F. Apply rub and mustard to both sides of the ribs as before. On each of the top sides, slather approximately 1 tablespoon of honey over the surface, then sprinkle heavily with about 2 tablespoons of turbinado sugar each. Lay the ribs meat side down on a piece of heavy-duty aluminum foil and fold up the edges. Pour 2 tablespoons of purple grape juice into the bottom of the foil for each rib then finish wrapping the ribs, but don't crimp the edges—you want steam to be able to escape.

(Continued on page 32)

For competitions, we ask our meat market to run the ribs through a band saw and lightly trim off the double bones and knuckles on the ends of the ribs. We also trim all meat and fat from the top of the ribs except for the cross-grain that runs across the middle. These steps help create a more consistent size for cooking and improve the appearance. If you are cooking at home, those steps aren't necessary.

Return the ribs to the cooker for 2 hours, then test for tenderness. (I cook ribs at this stage until they look overdone and too tender. Don't worry; they'll tighten up. If they still have too much texture, leave them in for 20 to 30 more minutes.) Remove the ribs from the cooker, open the foil, and drain off the liquid. Brush sauce on the bone side of the ribs. Then, using the foil as a tool, "roll" the ribs over so the meat side is up and glaze the tops. Using long tongs, carefully remove the ribs from the foil and place them back in the smoker for 15 minutes. This will let the glaze cook onto the ribs and let the ribs tighten back up. Remove from the cooker and allow to rest for 5 minutes, apply a very thin coat of glaze to "glisten" the ribs, then very lightly sprinkle with chipotle powder before serving.

PORK SPARERIBS

Serves 2 to 4

Outside of Memphis, where baby backs are predominate, spareribs are usually served in most restaurants. Spareribs are cut from the area closer to the belly (bacon) and as such have a richer, more "porky" flavor than baby backs. We serve St. Louis cut ribs, or spareribs with the breastbone area trimmed off, as they cook more consistently.

2 slabs St. Louis spareribs, about 3 pounds each

¾ cup Ultimate BBQ Rub (page 14)

¼ cup plus 2 tablespoons yellow mustard

1 cup Italian salad dressing

1 cup packed light brown sugar

½ cup honey

1 tablespoon Pickapeppa Sauce (see Notes)

½ cup Chipotle Bold BBQ Sauce (page 22)

½ cup Ultimate BBQ Rub (page 14) in a shaker with very small holes (see Notes)

Rinse the ribs and remove the membrane from the back. Trim any excess fat from the tops of the slabs. Starting on the backs, sprinkle the ribs with approximately 1 tablespoon of rub each, then spread on 1½ teaspoons mustard each and massage into the meat. Flip the ribs over and repeat. Wrap tightly in plastic wrap and refrigerate for 8 to 12 hours.

Prepare a smoker to cook at 250°F with cherry and pecan wood. Remove the ribs from the refrigerator, unwrap, and repeat the rub and mustard procedure, massaging them in. Don't get it too thick or pastelike, as this will give you a dark appearance when cooked. Place the ribs in the smoker meat side up and cook for 2½ hours, using a barbecue mop to lightly baste the tops of the ribs with Italian dressing every 30 minutes. Remove the ribs from the smoker and increase the temperature to 275°F.

Apply rub and mustard to both sides of the ribs as before. Tear off a large sheet of heavy-duty aluminum foil for each slab of ribs and sprinkle half of the brown sugar in the area where you will put the ribs, then drizzle half of the honey and half of the Pickapeppa Sauce over the sugar on each slab of ribs. Place the ribs meat side down directly into the sugar mix, then close the foil over the ribs, but don't crimp the edges; you want steam to escape.

Return to the smoker for 2 hours. Open the foil and check for tenderness. The ribs should be tender but still have texture. Remove from the smoker, open the foil, and drain, then remove from the foil. Sauce the back sides of the ribs, then flip over and sauce the top sides. Carefully return to the smoker for 15 minutes to tighten up the glaze, then remove and allow to rest for 5 to 10 minutes. Slice the ribs into serving portions, lightly dust with Ultimate BBQ Rub, and serve.

NOTES

If you can't find Pickapeppa Sauce, just sprinkle an additional ½ tablespoon of rub over the sugar.

When cooking for competition, you really have to make your product stand out in only one bite. I always keep some of my rub in a shaker with very small holes on top. After the meat is done cooking, lightly shake your rub over the ribs. The fine holes will let only a light dusting come through, so you will get added flavor without changing the appearance.

I LIKE PIG BUTTS! (AND I CANNOT LIE!)

Makes 3 to 4 pounds pulled pork, enough for 12 to 16 sandwiches

Pork butt is really kind of misnamed. It has nothing to do with what people consider a butt (on a hog, that would be the ham), but rather is the upper portion of the pork shoulder containing the blade bone (the lower portion is called the picnic and contains more bone and fat). We cook more than 6 tons of Boston butts a week at the restaurants, so I truly love them. They really become a sublime treat when cooked properly into Memphis-style pulled pork. You can also use it in Pulled Pork Quesadilla with Mango Salsa (page 43) or Pork Tamales (page 44).

1 (8- to 10-pound) pork butt

1½ cups Pork Competition Injection (page 18)

5 tablespoons Basic BBQ Rub (page 13), plus 1 tablespoon, optional

About ¼ cup mustard

⅓ cup turbinado sugar

½ cup Memphis-Style Vinegar Sauce (page 24), plus more for serving

Place the pork butt, fat side down, in an aluminum cooking pan. Using a small injection needle, inject the butt using a checkerboard pattern. You should be able to inject approximately 1½ cups of the injection, but if not, pour any remaining injection over the butt. Cover and refrigerate for at least 4 hours and up to overnight.

Prepare a smoker to cook at 250°F. I love to mix cherry and apple wood for smoke when I'm doing pork—about 4 to 6 chunks of each.

(Continued on page 39)

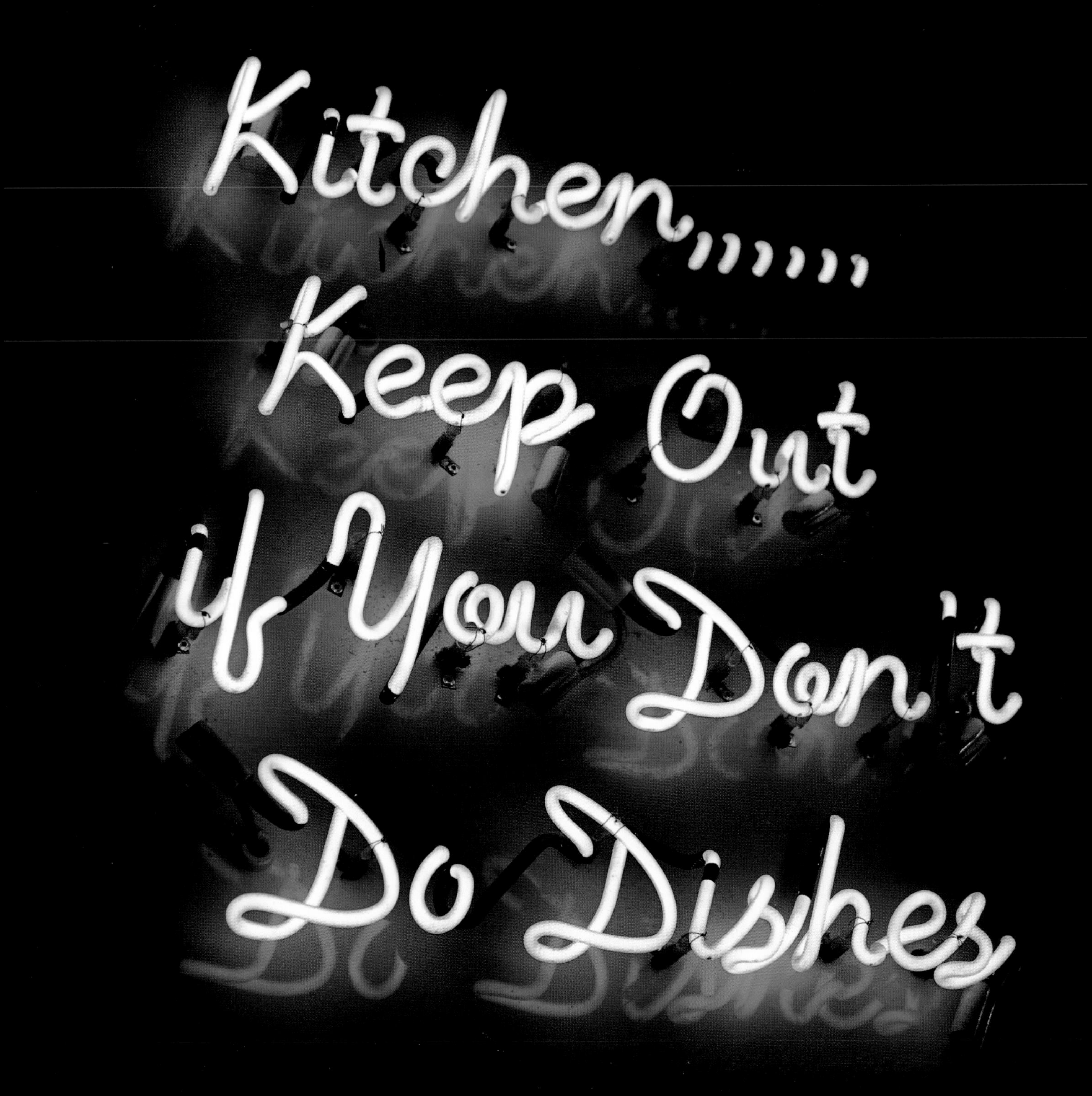
Kitchen,,,,,,
Keep Out
if You Don't
Do Dishes

The Memphis-Style
BARBECUE
SANDWICH

What makes a Memphis-style sandwich? Tender pulled pork like this, a rich flavorful sauce like our BBQ Mother Sauce (page 20), and a good helping of creamy coleslaw (page 129) on a good old-fashioned plain bun. (When you see some chefy type trying to sell you a barbecue sandwich on a "hearth-baked onion-sesame brioche bun," you know he or she's not from Memphis!) ★

Liberally sprinkle 2 tablespoons of the rub on the meat side of the butt, then spread about 3 tablespoons of mustard in a zigzag pattern over the top. Lovingly massage the butt. Remove from the pan and place in the smoker and cook for 4½ hours.

Remove the butt and place it on 2 sheets of heavy-duty aluminum foil that are about 2 feet long and arranged in a crisscross pattern. Sprinkle on 2 tablespoons of the remaining rub and then spread on about 1 more tablespoon of mustard. Rub in the mustard, then sprinkle with the turbinado sugar. Wrap up each piece of foil to fully enclose the butt and return it to the smoker for 4½ hours or until the internal temperature registers 195°F on a meat thermometer. If you like more "bark" on the outside of the pork, open the foil and sprinkle on an additional tablespoon of rub before the last hour of cooking. Place the butt (still wrapped) in a pan and poke a hole in the foil to drain off excess grease. Allow to rest in a Cambro or cooler for 1 to 2 hours.

Wearing heat-resistant gloves (see page 4), hand-pull the pork apart. Add the remaining tablespoon of rub and ½ cup of sauce and massage into the pork. Serve with additional sauce on the side.

CHAMPIONSHIP WHOLE PORK SHOULDER

Serves 10 to 12

One of the things that always surprises people is that my competition recipes are not really very complicated. What wins on the competition circuit is pretty close to what will win the battle of the backyards—great-tasting food! We have used this recipe on the circuit for years with great success. Serve it on a sandwich or use it in Pulled Pork Quesadilla with Mango Salsa (page 43) or Pork Tamales (page 44).

1 (18-pound) whole pork shoulder
3 cups Pork Competition
   Injection (page 18)
¼ cup Ultimate BBQ Rub
   (page 14)
2 tablespoons yellow mustard
2 tablespoons turbinado sugar
1 cup Sweet Glaze (page 21)

Place the shoulder on a flat surface fat side up. Using a sharp knife, score the fat across the shoulder, starting about 8 inches from the end of the shank. This should leave a "sleeve" around the shank bone. With the blade bone facing you, begin to remove the fat by slicing between the fat and the meat. Take your time and try to remove as little meat as possible. I keep this side up throughout the cooking process.

Place the shoulder in an aluminum pan and inject the pork injection throughout the shoulder. I especially like to concentrate on injecting down into the shoulder along the large shank bone and underneath the collar into the knuckle meat. Cover and refrigerate for at least 4 hours and up to overnight.

Prepare a smoker to cook at 225°F with 75 percent cherry wood and 25 percent hickory wood. Spread the wood across your charcoal so it will continue to smoke as the charcoal burns, and replenish the supply as needed. The first 6 hours should be very smoke intense. After 6 hours, I don't use any more wood chunks

Remove the shoulder from the refrigerator and sprinkle the side that had the fat with 2 tablespoons of the rub, then spread on about 1 tablespoon of the yellow mustard and massage into the meat. Clean off any rub from the collar and then heavily spray the collar with canola oil.

Remove the shoulder from the pan, place it in the smoker, and cook for 6 hours under constant smoke, recoating the collar with canola oil spray every 2 hours. Remove from the smoker and place it on 2 sheets of heavy-duty aluminum foil that are about 2 feet long and arranged in a crisscross pattern. Sprinkle with the remaining 2 tablespoons of rub, then apply the remaining 1 tablespoon of mustard and massage it into the meat. Sprinkle with the turbinado sugar, then wrap up the foil, but don't crimp the edges—you want steam to escape.

Return to the smoker and increase the temperature to 235°F. Continue to cook for 7 to 8 hours, or until the internal temperature registers 195°F on a meat thermometer. Decrease the temperature to 220°F, then poke a hole in the bottom of the foil and allow the rendered fat to drain. Carefully remove the foil from the shoulder, glaze it, and return it to the smoker for 10 minutes. Remove the shoulder, allow it to rest for 1 to 2 hours, then unwrap it. Use heat-resistant gloves (see page 4) to hand-pull the meat before serving.

SLATHERED COUNTRY-STYLE PORK RIBS

Serves 4

Country-style ribs are typically cut from the blade end of the pork loin next to the shoulder, although I've seen several different cuts labeled "country-style." Generally speaking, they don't contain "ribs," but they do have bones from the same end of the loin. The high fat content keeps the meat moist, and they respond very well to braising. My mother would put a mess of these in the roasting pan and cook them all day long at low temps, and the end result would be delicious, tender meat and an aroma that would drive you wild. This is one of my favorite comfort meals. Paired with mashed potatoes, it makes for a happy, happy dinner.

2 pounds country-style ribs

¼ cup Delta Creole Seasoning
(page 15)

2 cups BBQ Mother Sauce
(page 20)

Prepare a smoker to cook at 250°F with 2 to 3 chunks of cherry wood. Season the ribs all over with Delta Creole Seasoning, then place them in the smoker. Cook for 1 hour, then remove and place in an aluminum pan. Pour the sauce over the ribs, cover the pan tightly with heavy-duty aluminum foil, and return to the smoker for 4½ to 5 hours or until the internal temperature of the meat is 185°F and the meat is tender. Remove from the cooker and serve.

PULLED PORK QUESADILLA WITH MANGO SALSA

Serves 1 or 2

Super simple and satisfying, this is a great use for some leftover pulled pork.

SALSA

1 mango, peeled, pitted, and diced

½ cup peeled and diced cucumber

1 tablespoon finely diced jalapeño

⅓ cup diced red onion

⅓ cup diced red bell pepper

1 teaspoon canola oil

2 tablespoons finely chopped fresh cilantro

½ teaspoon granulated garlic

¼ teaspoon ground cumin

Salt and freshly ground black pepper

QUESADILLA

1 (9-inch) flour tortilla

⅓ cup mixed shredded cheese

⅓ cup pulled pork (page 36 or 40)

1 tablespoon diced yellow onion

1 tablespoon diced green bell pepper

1 teaspoon Fajita Seasoning (page 16)

To make the salsa, combine all the ingredients in a colander, mix well, and allow to drain while you make the quesadilla.

Oil a griddle and heat over medium-high heat. Lay the tortilla on the griddle, then spread the cheese in a half-moon pattern over half of the tortilla. Sprinkle on the pulled pork, onion, bell pepper, and the fajita seasoning, then fold the empty half of the tortilla over. Cook for 1 to 2 minutes, then flip over and cook for 1 to 2 minutes more, until golden brown. Serve with the salsa.

PORK TAMALES

Serves 6 to 10

My version of tamales uses leftover pulled pork and then braises that down some more to achieve a more familiar tamale texture. I like to skip the braising sometimes and just toss the pork with a little barbecue sauce before using it to fill the tamales. Traditional tamale dough uses lard, but I prefer shortening.

You'll need 48 pieces of 4- by 6-inch butcher paper or 48 dried corn husks (available at markets that carry Mexican ingredients).

PORK MIXTURE

½ cup canola oil

4 pounds pulled pork (page 36 or 40), roughly chopped

¼ cup light chili powder

2 tablespoons kosher salt

1 tablespoon onion powder

1 tablespoon granulated garlic

1 tablespoon coarsely ground black pepper

1 teaspoon cayenne

1 teaspoon ancho chile powder

1 teaspoon ground cumin

DOUGH

8 cups masa harina

1 tablespoon plus 1 teaspoon baking powder

2 teaspoons salt

1⅔ cups solid vegetable shortening

Heat the canola oil in a large stockpot over medium heat, then add the pork, chili powder, salt, onion powder, granulated garlic, pepper, cayenne, ancho, and cumin and stir until mixed well and warm, about 5 minutes. Add enough water to cover the pork by 2 inches. Cook for 1½ to 2 hours or until the pork is very, very tender. Remove the pork, but leave the cooking liquid in the pot.

To make the dough, stir the masa harina, baking powder, salt, and shortening together in a large bowl. Stir in hot cooking liquid about ½ cup at a time to make a soft dough. The dough should be moist, not wet, and the consistency should be like thick mashed potatoes. You will need approximately 4 cups of liquid. Leave the remaining braising liquid in the pot.

To assemble, lay a sheet of butcher paper in your hand and spoon approximately ¼ cup of the dough in an even layer on the sheet, leaving about 1 inch of space around the edges of the paper. Spoon about 1 tablespoon of the filling in a line down the center of the dough, then fold the paper so the dough goes over the filling and forms a roll. Fold up the bottom and set aside while you repeat with the remaining dough and filling.

Gather the tamales in groups of 6 to 8, stand them up together, and tie them loosely with a piece of butcher twine to form a bundle. Place them back in the stockpot so they are standing up. The braising liquid should be close to the top of the tamales, but add water if necessary. Bring to a boil, cover, decrease the heat to low, and simmer until the dough is firm, about 1 hour.

NOTE

The Delta never truly developed its own unique food items. Instead, it took foods from other traditions and added some soul to them. Tamales are found all over the Mississippi Delta now, and unlike their Mexican cousins, they are usually wrapped in butcher paper instead of corn husks. "Wet or dry?" is the common question in the tamale shops and barbecue joints that serve them. Wet means an extra ladle of the flavorful braising liquid spooned over the tamales. In the Delta, tamales are usually served with crackers. (Don't knock it 'til ya try it!)

GRILLED PORK T-BONES WITH BBQ BUTTER

Serves 4

Just like beef T-bones, pork T-bones contain a lower piece of the loin (the strip loin section of a beef T-bone) and a section of the tenderloin (the filet of the pig). I treat this simply: well seasoned, grilled to medium, and then topped with a thick pat of my BBQ Butter. Delish! The BBQ Butter can be made ahead and frozen. Just pull out a portion a couple of hours before needed. I also love to use it to top steaks, chops, and even breads for a nifty treat.

BBQ BUTTER

1 pound (4 sticks) unsalted butter, softened

2 tablespoons minced garlic

1 tablespoon lemon juice

2 tablespoons finely diced red bell pepper

1½ teaspoons Basic BBQ Rub (page 13)

½ teaspoon kosher salt

½ teaspoon coarsely ground black pepper

PORK T-BONES

4 pork T-bones, each 1½ inches thick (see Note)

¼ cup Grill Seasoning (page 17)

Place the butter in the bowl of a stand mixer and add the remaining butter ingredients. Using the paddle attachment, mix on low-medium for 3 to 4 minutes, scraping the bowl a couple of times, until well incorporated. Divide into 4 portions, lay each on an 8-inch square of parchment paper, and roll up into a log shape. Wrap tightly in plastic wrap and freeze until firm. The butter will keep in the freezer for up to 3 months.

Prepare a medium-hot grill and oil the grates. Season the T-bones with about 2 tablespoons of the grill seasoning each, then place on the grill and cook for 3 to 4 minutes per side or until medium. Remove from the grill and allow to rest for 5 minutes, then serve with a pat of butter on each.

NOTE

Pork chops of a similar thickness may be substituted.

PEPPERED PORK TENDERLOIN WITH HOECAKES *and* MISSISSIPPI CAVIAR

Serves 4

Pork tenderloin is one of the most versatile cuts of meat available. It serves as a wonderful palette for any number of flavors, from Mexican to Asian and all places in between. This version has the snap of cracked black pepper set off against a jalapeño hoecake and cooling Mississippi caviar. Hoecakes are basically corn bread pancakes. They get their name from field workers who would cook them on the flat metal of the hoe over a fire. They're a wonderful quick bread that you can make while grilling your entrée. In fact, if you prepare the caviar in advance and heat your griddle while the tenderloin is grilling, you can cook the hoecakes while the meat rests and serve dinner in 20 minutes.

MISSISSIPPI CAVIAR

2 cups drained cooked black-eyed peas

1 cup fresh whole-kernel corn (see page 145)

1 cup diced tomato

1 tablespoon diced fresh jalapeño (optional)

1 tablespoon chopped fresh cilantro

1½ teaspoons canola oil

½ teaspoon salt

¼ teaspoon granulated garlic

½ teaspoon ground cumin

PORK

2 teaspoons coarsely ground black pepper

1 teaspoon dried thyme

½ teaspoon kosher salt

1 teaspoon granulated garlic

2 (1-pound) pork tenderloins, trimmed of excess fat and silverskin (see Note, page 50)

2 tablespoons Dijon mustard

HOECAKES

2 cups self-rising white cornmeal

¾ cup self-rising flour

½ cup finely diced yellow onion

¼ cup finely diced pickled jalapeño

1½ teaspoons salt

2 large eggs, lightly beaten

2 cups buttermilk

2 tablespoons canola oil, or as needed

(Continued on page 50)

To make the caviar, combine all the ingredients in a small mixing bowl, mix well, and refrigerate for at least 2 hours before serving and up to overnight.

For the pork, prepare a medium-hot grill. Combine the pepper, thyme, salt, and granulated garlic in a small bowl and mix well. Cut each tenderloin in half crosswise, massage them with mustard, then lightly sprinkle with the seasoning mix. Lightly oil the grates on the prepared grill, then place the tenderloin pieces on the grates and cook for 12 to 15 minutes, turning every 2 minutes or so, until the internal temperature reaches 140°F on a meat thermometer. Remove from the grill, cover with aluminum foil, and rest for 5 to 7 minutes while you cook the hoecakes.

In a medium mixing bowl, stir together the cornmeal, flour, onion, jalapeño, salt, eggs, and buttermilk. Place a griddle on the grill, add the oil, and heat. Using a large spoon, drop about ¼ cup of the batter onto the griddle and allow to form a pancake shape. Cook for 2 to 3 minutes, flip, and cook for 2 minutes longer or until golden and cooked through. As the hoecakes will absorb the oil, you may need to add more to the griddle after each batch. Repeat with the remaining batter until you have at least 8 hoecakes.

To serve, place 2 hoecakes on each plate. Slice the tenderloin approximately ½ inch thick on a bias and arrange in a shingle pattern across the hoecakes. Top with 1 tablespoon of caviar and serve.

NOTE

Silverskin is a tough membrane on the surface of tenderloins and loins of most meats (pork, lamb, beef, etc.). Use a very sharp filleting knife to remove it to allow better texture and to let the flavors get further into your meats.

SMOKIN' A FATTIE

Serves 4 to 6 as an appetizer

Fattie is the common term for a smoked, stuffed breakfast sausage. This is one of those items I like to start when I'm putting in something else to smoke because it's easy, it tastes great, and it makes for a very interesting appetizer. This is really a "kitchen sink" dish—stuff it with about anything you want and it'll be pretty fine!

1 tablespoon canola oil

½ cup slivered yellow onion

½ cup slivered green bell pepper

½ cup sliced portobello mushroom

1 pound sage breakfast sausage

1½ tablespoons Ultimate BBQ Rub (page 14)

1 cup shredded mozzarella cheese

½ cup crispy cooked bacon bits, made from Makin' Bacon (page 66) or your favorite brand

¼ cup Chipotle Bold BBQ Sauce (page 22)

Set up a smoker to cook at 250°F using 3 or 4 chunks of cherry or other fruit wood.

Heat the canola oil in a small skillet and sauté the onion, bell pepper, and mushroom until soft, about 4 minutes. Place the sausage in a 1-gallon resealable plastic bag and press it out to form a ½-inch layer. Cut off the top of the bag along the edges, but leave the sausage on the bottom piece of the bag. Sprinkle the sausage with 1½ teaspoons of the rub, then spread the pepper mixture across the middle of the sausage, leaving about 1 inch around the edges, followed by the cheese and bacon bits. Using the plastic bag as a tool, roll up the sausage and press it together to seal. Season the outside of the sausage roll with the remaining 1 tablespoon of rub and place it in the smoker for 2 hours. Remove from the smoker, lightly coat with the barbecue sauce, rest for 5 minutes, then slice and serve.

SMOKED PORK LOIN WITH BLACKBERRY CHUTNEY

Serves 3 to 4

I spent many a summer day crawling through weeds and fighting off chiggers and snakes just to pick a bucket of luscious blackberries. Blackberries are the flavor of my youth, and I still try to sneak out in June, when the berries are at their plumpest and juiciest, and pick a few to make into cobblers and jellies. This chutney uses blackberries to bring a rich sweetness and beautiful contrast to the pork.

BLACKBERRY CHUTNEY

- 1 tablespoon olive oil
- 1 medium red onion, finely chopped
- 1 tablespoon finely chopped fresh ginger
- 1 teaspoon minced garlic
- 2 jalapeños, finely diced (seeds removed for a milder chutney)
- 1 pound fresh blackberries
- ⅓ cup sugar
- 2 tablespoons red wine vinegar

PORK LOIN

- 1 (3- to 4-pound) boneless pork loin
- 3 tablespoons Grill Seasoning (page 17)
- 2 tablespoons whole-grain mustard

To make the chutney, heat the olive oil in a small saucepan. Add the onion, ginger, and garlic and cook for 4 to 5 minutes, until the onion is translucent. Add the jalapeño and blackberries and cook for 4 minutes. Add the sugar and vinegar and bring to a boil, then decrease the heat and simmer for 8 to 10 minutes, stirring occasionally. You'll serve it hot here, but it can be stored in the refrigerator for up to 1 week and reheated for serving.

Prepare a smoker to cook at 250°F with cherry wood. Rinse the pork loin and trim off the silverskin and excess fat. Sprinkle with the grill seasoning, slather with the mustard, and massage it into the loin.

Place the loin in the smoker and cook for 2 hours or until the internal temperature registers 150°F on a meat thermometer. Remove from the smoker, cover with aluminum foil, and allow to rest for 10 to 15 minutes. To serve, slice into 1-inch chops and top each with a tablespoon of hot chutney.

WHOLE HOG

Makes 40 to 50 pounds of meat, serving a whole lot of folks

When we were newlyweds, my husband took me to my first barbecue contest. We watched quite a few teams and talked with many. Without fail, they all mentioned cooking whole hog as being the most challenging thing in barbecue. Right then and there I decided I wanted to cook it.

It was a long road from the first hog we cooked to winning the Memphis in May World Championship in 2010. We had varying degrees of success, and it took quite a few years to fully develop our cooking methods and achieve the textures and flavors we wanted. While smoking whole hogs isn't for everyone, since it's what I became known for, I just had to include my method here for those with the equipment and the desire to try it. Cooking a whole hog is about time, patience, friendship, and fellowship. It takes a long time and a night with only some cat naps in between checking on the grill, but the finished product tastes amazing.

Whole hog is a challenge not merely because of the size but also because of the variety of muscles, textures, differences in thicknesses, and time involved. But hey, that's what makes it fun! There are two main ways of cooking it: running style, which means the hog is belly down while cooking, and the more common belly-up style. Before you decide which method to use, you need to be cognizant of the pit that you are cooking on. If it's a direct-fired type of cooker (or a concrete pit), belly-up is the only way to go to minimize the chance of pit fires. (I have had a pig catch on fire, and it's not a pleasant experience!) I cook on indirect water cookers, but there are many types available that will do the job, from homemade barrels to high-end cookers. Don't let the cooker dissuade you. If it's big enough and you can control it, you can cook a whole hog.

Before you embark on this endeavor, remember first that no two hogs are alike. Some are long and lean (what the meat industry prefers breeding, generally called *loin-hogs*) and some are short and squat. Always go for short and squat if you can. Second, the entire cooking process is driven by the shoulders. Basically, your goal is to get the shoulders tender without overcooking the loins and hams. This is best accomplished by placing the hog in your cooker and directing the heat flow away from the loins and hams as much as possible.

The following method is for a belly-up style. For competitions, we cook a modified running-style hog with a whole lot of trimming. Though I've prepared literally thousands of hogs that way, it still takes me 2 to 3 hours each time. This method is significantly easier to prepare, you still get a good-quality result, and I have won several Grand Championships cooking a hog in exactly this manner. Frankly, 95 percent of the competitors cook a belly-up hog in contests for those very reasons. Even though this way is easier, you definitely need some helpers around to prepare the hog and move it to the (large) cooker.

The timing and temperature for this recipe is based on cooking a 150-pound pig, so you may need to adjust for smaller or larger pigs.

1 (150-pound) whole hog, cleaned
(see Note, page 58)

4 quarts Pork Competition
Injection (page 18)

2½ cups Ultimate BBQ Rub
(page 14)

1 cup yellow mustard

Canola oil spray

2 cups Sweet Glaze (page 21)

Prepare a smoker to cook at 225°F with 70 percent of your fruit wood of choice and 30 percent hickory wood. The number of chunks will depend on the size of your smoker.

If your hog is already butterflied with the feet removed, skip this step. Otherwise, start by laying the hog on its back on a sturdy prep table. Mark the legs between the shoulder joint and the elbow joint and use a boning knife to slice through the skin and fat all the way around the bone. Using a hacksaw or a reciprocating saw, slice through the bone to remove the feet. Have a helper stand by the head and hold the chest cavity open, then place the saw blade against the backbone and cut down to a point approximately 12 inches from the tail. Be very careful not to cut all the way through the skin—you are basically scoring the backbone and pulling it open. Using a very sharp boning knife, slice approximately 1 inch off the belly, trimming off the nipples. Using the knife, cut between the bacon and the skin about 2 inches deep to form a pocket. Trim excess fat away from the shoulders. Pull the interior fat from the inside of the belly and expose the tenderloins. Trim any excess fat from the hams.

Using a large injector, inject the hams and shoulders. I spend extra time and make sure the injection hits around the bone. I don't inject the loins, as the injection will force open the fibers of this lean cut and make it more apt to break apart when cooked. Instead, I inject around them to add some moisture. Pour any remaining injection on either side of the backbone.

Use your hand to rub that excess injection over the meat, then sprinkle approximately 1 cup of the rub over the surface and into the slits you cut by the bacon. Using about ½ cup of the mustard, massage in the seasoning. Lay 2 sheets of heavy-duty aluminum foil in the smoker, covering the area where you will place the hog. With your helpers, place the hog in the smoker. Dampen a towel and clean off any rub that got on the skin, then heavily coat any exposed skin with the nonstick

(Continued on page 56)

cooking spray. Take a piece of wood approximately 1½ to 2 inches thick and prop up the sides of the belly to form a bowl. Insert a meat thermometer into the shoulders and another one into the hams, taking care not to get too close to the bones.

Close the smoker and cook for 6 hours, replenishing the wood to keep smoke on the pig constantly and recoating the skin with nonstick spray every 2 hours. After 3 hours, lay a piece of foil over the backbone/loin area and fold it to hold it in place. Lay another sheet over the hams. Repeat the rub and mustard massage with the same amounts. Tear off several large sheets of foil and begin to wrap the hog by first laying a strip over the backbone and folding it to cover the loin area, then wrapping the entire pig with foil, first lengthwise and then across, to help tuck in the foil. Close the smoker and increase the temperature to 260°F. Cook for 12 hours, checking the temperature occasionally. The pig will hit a "wall" as the temperature nears 160°F and will

probably spend 2 to 3 hours hovering right around that temperature, then will continue to rise. The goal is to get the shoulders to 185°F and the hams to 175°F. To this day, I have never put a temperature probe in a loin. The basic premise on a hog is to try to get the shoulders and hams done and leave the loins as low as you possibly can, as they are much leaner and will overcook.

Remove a section of foil over the shoulders and give it the finger test: The meat should be soft to the touch, and your finger should leave a small impression, but the meat should not break apart. If the meat feels too firm, re-cover and continue to cook, checking it each hour. If it is ready, unwrap the foil, and drain the liquid from the bowl formed by the belly by either transferring it with a dipper or poking a small hole through the belly. Lightly sprinkle the meat with some or all of the remaining ½ cup of rub and cook for an additional 30 minutes to tighten up the meat and set the bark. Glaze the meat with sauce and allow to rest in the cooker for 30 minutes. The hog is ready to serve!

NOTE

If you are not comfortable with power tools, or just to save a step, ask your local meat market to prepare the hog by butterflying it and trimming off the feet. I like to do that myself, as I get to use a reciprocating saw!

NOTES ON SERVING

1. It's helpful to wear a pair of cotton gloves with nitrile gloves over them while pulling the hot meat (see page 4).

2. Using your fingers, separate the ends of the ribs and push up to fold them inward to expose the loin.

3. The muscle directly at the bottom of the ham is the most tender and delicious muscle on the hog. You will be able to feel the difference between it and the surrounding muscles. As the cook, you deserve first crack at this!

4. Run your fingers between the skin and the bacon and then fold the whole piece inward. Reach into this and pull the large sheets of muscle up, then, using a knife, scrape the fat from the meat. This is whole-hog bacon and is absolutely luscious.

5. You should be able to reach into the loin and, by running your hands up and down, separate the loin and remove it in basically one piece. Sprinkle a little rub on it, then slice it into medallions.

6. The tenderloin usually takes on a "cured" texture as it is very thin. It is still delicious when removed and sliced into medallions and sauced.

TASSO HAM

Makes 4 to 5 pounds

Tasso ham is typically not eaten as ham but is used to accent dishes and season stews and gumbos. I love it and use it often in a lot of my cooking. "Green" or fresh hams are fairly hard to find, so I mainly use a Boston butt for this recipe—it really gives it a nice texture. It takes 8 days to prepare, but it's worth it. I make one at a time, then cut it into chunks and freeze what I can't use quickly.

4 quarts water
1¾ cups sugar cure (see Note)
1½ cups Delta Creole Seasoning (page 15)
1½ cups granulated sugar
½ cup kosher salt
1 (8- to 10-pound) pork Boston butt
1 teaspoon cayenne
1 tablespoon ground sage

Place the water, sugar cure, ½ cup of the seasoning, the sugar, and the salt in a large stockpot, bring to a boil, and boil until the sugar is dissolved. Remove the brine from the heat and allow to cool.

Cut the pork butt in half, remove the blade bone, place the butt in a plastic container, and pour the brine over it. Place a plate over the butt to keep it immersed, then cover and refrigerate for 7 days. Discard the brine and thoroughly rinse the pork butt.

Prepare a smoker to cook at 200°F with 4 to 6 chunks each of apple and pecan wood. Mix the remaining 1 cup of seasoning with the cayenne and dried sage and pack it onto the butt. Tasso should have a thick crust of seasoning. Place in the smoker for 12 hours or until it reaches an internal temperature of 185°F. Allow to cool, then use in recipes as a great flavor booster.

NOTE

We use cures in several recipes, and they may not be available at your local supermarket. I order sugar cure from online sources, though your local butcher shop may be able to provide it for you.

RACK OF LAMB

Serves 4 to 6

We won the Exotic category at Memphis in May with this dish one year. Keep a meat thermometer nearby when cooking, as the thin rack can go from beautiful to overcooked very quickly.

MARINADE

½ cup olive oil

1 tablespoon red wine vinegar

1 tablespoon minced garlic

1 tablespoon fresh rosemary, coarsely chopped

1 tablespoon chopped fresh parsley

1 tablespoon kosher salt

1 tablespoon coarsely ground black pepper

1 teaspoon fresh oregano, coarsely chopped

5 or 6 fresh basil leaves, chopped

1 tablespoon fresh orange juice

LAMB

2 racks of lamb, frenched

2 tablespoons Ultimate BBQ Rub (page 14)

2 tablespoons whole-grain mustard

½ cup Chipotle Bold BBQ Sauce (page 22)

In a small bowl, whisk together the marinade ingredients. Place each rack of lamb in a large resealable plastic bag and divide the marinade between the bags. Seal tightly and refrigerate for 3 to 4 hours, turning the bags once or twice.

Prepare a smoker to cook at 185°F with cherry wood. Remove the lamb from the bags, discard the marinade, sprinkle the meat with the rub, then massage the mustard into the meat. Clean and dry the bones, then cover them with aluminum foil. Place in the smoker and cook for 45 minutes. Meanwhile, heat a grill to medium-hot. Remove the lamb from the smoker and place it on the grill. Cook for 3 to 4 minutes per side or until the internal temperature registers 145°F on a meat thermometer. Glaze with the sauce.

Remove from the grill, allow to rest for 4 or 5 minutes, then slice between the bones to form chops.

Bacon has become all the rage everywhere of late, but in the Delta it has always been the star of the show. Most people love bacon, and a whole contingent of folks are putting bacon in just about any dish you could think of making. I grew up in the country, and the fall was always hog-harvesting time. Hogs would be cleaned, butchered, and literally every part used in some form or fashion. The thick slabs of bacon would be cured and hung in the smokehouse for days as people put up bacon for the winter. This was the original organic/locavore movement—food raised and prepared locally and utilized "from squeal to heel"— and bacon was always everyone's favorite part. Commercially prepared bacon will work in a pinch, but if you really want bacon with beautiful smoky goodness, try your hand at curing and smoking your own.

4

BACON

MAKIN' BACON

Makes about 8 pounds

One of the things we are constantly doing in the restaurants is preparing bacon. There is literally always around 1 ton of pork bellies in the restaurants in some phase of the bacon-curing process. Though it can be a little time consuming, bacon is simple to make, and it has a much richer flavor than you can get from store-bought bacon. Fresh pork bellies can be a challenge to buy, but your local meat market can usually order them for you.

1 whole fresh pork belly
1 cup sugar cure (see Note)
1 cup packed light brown sugar
½ cup Basic BBQ Rub (page 13)
½ cup coarsely ground black pepper (optional)

Cut the pork belly into 4 equal pieces. Liberally sprinkle each piece with sugar cure and then the brown sugar, making sure to coat each piece on all sides. Place all the pieces in a container, cover tightly, and refrigerate for 2 days. Rotate the pieces, re-cover, and cure for 3 more days, for a total of 5. Remove the pieces and wash each thoroughly under cold water. Washing removes the cure and keeps the bacon from being too salty. Liberally sprinkle with the rub; add the pepper if you want a pepper bacon.

Prepare a smoker to cook at 175°F using 3 to 4 chunks of your favorite wood. We prefer to use pecan for bacon, but cherry, apple, or hickory will work as well. Place the bacon in the smoker and cook for 8 hours, replenishing the wood as necessary.

After smoking, wrap the bacon pieces in plastic wrap and refrigerate overnight. You need to do this to firm it up before slicing. Slice to the desired thickness and cook as you would cook store-bought bacon.

You can place unused bacon on wax paper, roll it up, wrap it in plastic wrap, and freeze, as it keeps very well. I like to wrap it in 1-pound increments so I know how much I am taking out of the freezer at any time. It will keep in the freezer for up to 2 months.

NOTE

We use cures in several recipes, and they may not be available at your local supermarket. I order sugar cure from online sources, though your local butcher shop may be able to provide it for you.

BLT WITH SMOKED TOMATO JAM

Makes 1 sandwich

The smoked tomato jam brings an amplified savory note to this standby, taking it to a whole new level.

6 slices Makin' Bacon (page 66) or your favorite brand

2 slices Texas toast

1 tablespoon Smoked Tomato Jam (recipe follows)

1 or 2 fresh lettuce leaves

1 tomato, sliced

Lay the strips of bacon in a large skillet over medium heat and cook until rendered and crisp. Transfer to a paper-towel-lined plate to drain.

Lightly toast the bread, then spread tomato jam on each half. Top with the lettuce, tomato slices, and bacon.

SMOKED TOMATO JAM

Makes about 4 cups

Tomato jam is a wonderfully savory sweet concoction. I like to smoke my tomatoes to add an additional layer of flavor.

2 pounds heirloom or Roma tomatoes

¼ cup olive oil

1 tablespoon minced garlic

1 teaspoon freshly ground black pepper

3 cups sugar

¼ cup fresh lemon juice

½ teaspoon ground cumin

1 teaspoon kosher salt

1 teaspoon granulated garlic

1 teaspoon chipotle chile powder

Prepare a smoker to cook at 250°F. Core the tomatoes and cut them in half. In a small pan that will fit in your smoker, place the tomatoes cut side down. Drizzle with olive oil and sprinkle with the fresh garlic. Place in the smoker and cook for 2½ hours or until soft.

Pour the tomatoes and juice into a large stockpot with the pepper, sugar, lemon juice, cumin, salt, granulated garlic, and chipotle powder. Use an immersion blender to puree everything. Bring to a boil, then decrease the heat to simmer for 30 to 40 minutes or until the jam is thick. Remove from the heat, pour into a sealable container, and allow to cool. The jam will keep in the refrigerator for 5 days.

BACON CANDY

Makes 12 slices

This is AWESOME! The saltiness of the bacon, the savoriness of the seasoning, and the sweetness from the brown sugar make for a great treat. For an even richer taste, add 1 teaspoon of cayenne to the rub to increase the heat a little. You can use any type of bacon, but home-cured bacon really shines here. Leave the candy whole for a wonderful snack or break it into pieces to top a salad or mix into vanilla bean ice cream.

1 pound (about 12 slices) Makin' Bacon (page 66) or your favorite brand

1 tablespoon Basic BBQ Rub (page 13)

½ cup packed light brown sugar

Prepare a smoker to cook at 275°F. Place a sheet of parchment paper across a baking sheet. Lay the bacon slices across the pan, then sprinkle with rub and liberally cover with brown sugar.

Place in the smoker to cook for 30 minutes. The bacon candy should be fairly crisp and the sugar caramelized. If it is not getting crispy, leave in the cooker for 10 to 15 minutes longer. (Alternatively, you can place in a 325°F oven for 20 to 30 minutes.) Remove from the smoker and allow to cool before serving.

HOT BACON DRESSING

Makes about 4 cups

One of the downsides of making your own bacon is that you generate quite a bit of bacon ends and pieces that you can't slice very well. While those make the best bacon bits you could ever have, I've also included a couple of recipes to make use of these trimmings. This recipe uses those pieces to make a traditional hot dressing. Serve it over a spinach salad or use it to top lightly sautéed fresh green beans.

1 pound trimmings from Makin' Bacon (page 66) or your favorite brand

½ cup diced yellow onion

1 cup cider vinegar

2 cups water plus 2 tablespoons cold water

1½ cups sugar

2 tablespoons Dijon mustard

1 teaspoon salt

½ teaspoon coarsely ground black pepper

3 tablespoons cornstarch

In a large skillet over medium heat, cook the bacon pieces until rendered and crisp. Transfer the pieces to a paper-towel-lined plate to drain, and drain off all but 2 tablespoons of the bacon grease from the skillet. Add the onion to the skillet and cook until tender, then add the vinegar, the 2 cups of water, the sugar, mustard, salt, and pepper and stir. In a cup, stir together the cornstarch and the 2 tablespoons of cold water and then add to skillet. Bring to a boil for 2 minutes, then reduce to a simmer and add the bacon pieces (crumbling into bits if necessary). Serve warm.

MAPLE BACON JAM

Makes about 8 cups

This is a treat I allow myself occasionally. It's not your typical breakfast jam, as it's sweet, savory, and salty with a little heat from the serrano chiles. While it will still be mighty fine on a biscuit, I like to use this almost as a sauce with entrées. Try letting about 1½ teaspoons melt over pork loin medallions or a grilled chicken breast to give them additional flavor.

2 pounds trimmings from Makin' Bacon (page 66) or your favorite brand, diced
2 yellow onions, chopped
2 tablespoons minced garlic
1 serrano chile, diced
1 cup cider vinegar
1 cup brewed coffee
1 cup maple syrup
1 cup packed light brown sugar
1 teaspoon freshly ground black pepper
½ teaspoon ground cumin

In a medium saucepan, cook the bacon over medium heat until crispy, 7 to 8 minutes. Transfer the bacon to a paper-towel-lined plate to drain. Drain off all but around 1 tablespoon of the bacon grease. Add the onion to the pan and sauté for 4 to 5 minutes, then add the garlic and chile and sauté for 1 minute. Deglaze the pan with the vinegar, using a wooden spoon to scrape up any bits stuck to the bottom of the pan. Add the coffee, syrup, brown sugar, pepper, cumin, and bacon. Decrease the heat and simmer for 1 to 2 hours, until the liquid is reduced to a syrupy consistency. Pour into a food processor and pulse until it reaches a semi-smooth consistency. (You still want some texture.) Pour the jam into a sealable container and refrigerate. It will keep for up to 2 weeks.

I was raised on pork, but I am a sucker for beef. I absolutely love it. Maybe it's from only having beef on very special occasions when I was a child, but I almost never pass on the opportunity to sample brisket or enjoy a well-marbled steak. In fact, I know when my husband or daughter have been up to no good (just kidding, honey) when I get home to a prime ribeye grilling over coals with a big baked potato and some smoked Vidalias—they know me too well!

Brisket is the most common cut used for smoking, and I've included several recipes here for brisket (plus brisket chili, a great way to make something delicious out of leftovers). A whole brisket is composed of two parts, the flat and the point (also called the *deckle*). The flat, just like its name suggests, is a large flat muscle covered with a layer of fat. There is a layer of fat between the flat and the point as well. The point is a smaller muscle with a higher internal fat content. I always prefer cooking briskets whole, but you can get a wonderful product just cooking the flat. Bear in mind that in the supermarket, the premium price applied to the flat sometimes makes it more expensive than purchasing the entire brisket. As the point is typically juicier (and the part from which you make burnt ends!), if you have the room, go on and get the whole thing.

5
BEEF

BRISKET AT THE HOUSE *and* BURNT ENDS

Makes 4 to 5 pounds

There is a definite difference in my barbecue depending on whether I'm cooking at a contest or for family and friends. As with competition pork versus pork for the house, I am not as worried about one-bite flavor or pleasing the majority of judges' palates. When cooking at home, I can cook what my family and I love. This is a simple, old-school brisket complete with a rich, deep crust and a dense smoke flavor, and while I have turned in similar briskets and done well in competition, cooking this recipe is about expressing a more traditional flavor than most judges expect. You will have leftover rub, and it will keep in an airtight container for about a month.

HOUSE BRISKET RUB

1 cup kosher salt
½ cup granulated garlic
¼ cup coarsely ground black pepper

FOR THE BRISKET

1 (10- to 12-pound) choice-grade whole beef brisket
2½ tablespoons yellow mustard

FOR THE BURNT ENDS

2 tablespoons Ultimate BBQ Rub (page 14)
1 cup Chipotle Bold BBQ Sauce (page 22)

Prepare a smoker to cook at 250°F. I prefer pecan wood, but any milder wood will do. I use 4 to 6 chunks of wood through the first 3 hours, then replenish it. I don't use any more wood after I wrap the meat in foil.

Mix the ingredients for the house rub.

Remove any fat pockets from the surface of the flat part of the brisket and any surface fat from the top of the point. Sprinkle the meat side with 2 tablespoons of the rub, then top with 1½ tablespoons of the mustard and massage it into the meat. Place in the smoker meat side up and cook for 6 hours or until the internal temperature registers 150° to 160°F on a meat thermometer.

Remove the brisket and place it in large aluminum pan. Season with 1 more tablespoon of the house rub and the remaining 1 tablespoon of mustard and massage into the meat. Leave the brisket in the pan and return to the smoker. Cook until the internal temperature reaches 202°F or a meat probe slides in easily, 3 to 4 more hours. Remove from the smoker and allow to cool for 5 minutes. Pour off the drippings into another container and set aside. Using a sharp boning knife and wearing heatproof gloves (see page 4), slice through the fat between the point and the flat to separate the pieces. Leave the flat of the brisket in the pan, cover, and place in an empty cooler or Cambro for 1 to 2 hours to rest.

(Continued on page 76)

For the burnt ends, place the point of the brisket on a cutting board and remove the exterior fat. Slice horizontally through the middle of the point and then cut into 1-inch-square pieces. Place in a small pan, season with Ultimate BBQ Rub, and pour in ½ cup of the beef drippings and the sauce. Stir to coat the pieces. Place the uncovered pan back into the cooker for 1½ hours, or until the sauce is caramelized around the ends.

To serve the rest of the brisket, remove the flat from the pan, reserving any more accumulated drippings. Slice into ¼-inch slices across the grain and serve with the drippings. The brisket and the burnt ends will keep in resealable plastic bags in the freezer for up to 2 months.

COMPETITION BRISKET

Makes 4 to 5 pounds

When cooking briskets for competition, we aim for a few different attributes than when cooking at home. Contests can be decided by .01, so we focus on perfect texture, appearance, and a rich flavor but one that doesn't offend anyone (too sweet, too salty, etc.). This is the recipe we used to win the brisket category in the Kingsford Invitational.

1 (14- to 16-pound) whole prime-grade or Wagyu beef brisket

6 cups Beef Competition Injection (page 19)

¼ cup seasoned salt

¼ cup Ultimate BBQ Rub (page 14)

2 tablespoons finely ground black pepper

¼ cup yellow mustard

1 cup Memphis-Style Vinegar Sauce (page 24; optional)

Place the brisket on a cutting board fat side up. Trim the fat to an even layer (without cutting into the meat), then turn over and trim all fat pockets and sinew from the top of the meat. Identify the direction the grain is running and look for the thinnest part of the flat. I usually make a cut with the grain about 2 inches from the edge on the thinnest side of the flat, but don't cut all the way through. If you're cooking for a contest, this will help make your turn-in pieces more even but also give you some "sampling" pieces so you can adjust the flavor.

Place the brisket in a large aluminum pan and inject approximately 2 cups of the beef injection in a checkerboard pattern. Go slowly or the injection will run down the grain and shoot out the sides! Cover and chill for at least 4 hours.

Prepare a smoker to cook at 275°F. For competition brisket, I like to use cherry wood, as it will make a beautiful smoke ring at the top of the brisket. I use 4 to 6 chunks of wood and replenish as necessary for the first 6 hours of cooking. Sprinkle the top of the brisket with 2 tablespoons of salt, 2 tablespoons of rub, and 1 tablespoon of pepper. Spread on approximately 2 tablespoons of the mustard and lightly massage into the meat. Place the brisket in the smoker meat side up and cook for 4 hours. The meat should register approximately 160°F on a meat thermometer.

Remove from the smoker and place on 2 sheets of aluminum foil arranged in a crisscross pattern. Repeat the seasoning and mustard process, pour in approximately ½ cup of the remaining beef injection, wrap tightly, and return to the smoker. Cook until the internal temperature of the meat reaches 202°F and the probe slides in easily, 3½ to 4 hours. Remove from the smoker, open the foil, and allow to vent for 5 minutes before placing in an empty cooler or Cambro for at least 1 hour.

Heat the remaining 3½ cups of beef injection and pour into a serving pan. Place the brisket on a cutting board. Slice across the grain and check the taste and tenderness. If the tenderness is right, cut into slices approximately the width of a No. 2 pencil, or slightly thinner if the brisket is a little tough. Place the slices into the warm injection and allow to soak for 30 seconds. Remove and serve. Lightly glaze with the barbecue sauce, if desired.

PASTRAMI

Makes about 4 pounds

I really love to do things that take a little time—that alone seems to make the end result so much better! Couple that with the fact that I'm a sucker for a good pastrami sandwich, and you'll understand why I love this recipe so much.

1 (12-pound) whole beef brisket

CURE

¼ cup Morton Tender Quick Home Meat Cure

¼ cup packed dark brown sugar

¼ cup coarsely ground black pepper

3 tablespoons granulated garlic

2 tablespoons pickling spice

2 tablespoons ground coriander

PASTRAMI RUB

3 tablespoons coarsely ground black pepper

1 tablespoon coriander seeds, toasted and ground

1 teaspoon granulated garlic

1 cup water

Rinse the brisket. Using a knife, separate the point and the flat, then trim the fat to a uniform thickness. I like to leave on about ½ inch of fat.

Mix together all of the curing ingredients, then apply to all surfaces of the brisket. Place in a large sealable bag (2-gallon if possible, or use two 1-gallon bags). Refrigerate for 4 days, turning once or twice a day.

Remove the brisket from the bags and rinse very thoroughly. Pat dry. In a small mixing bowl, combine and mix the pastrami rub ingredients. Apply the rub to the brisket and allow to sit for 10 minutes. I season both sides, but more heavily on the meat side to form a light crust.

Prepare a smoker to cook at 230°F. I love cherry wood for this recipe, but pecan, oak, or apple is fine.

Place the pastrami cuts fat side up and cook for 4 to 5 hours or until the internal temperature on the thickest pieces registers 165°F. Remove from the smoker, place each piece on a double layer of heavy-duty aluminum foil, cup the foil, add ½ cup of water to each, and wrap tightly. Return to the smoker and cook until the internal temperature of the meat registers 180°F (for deli texture) or 195°F for melt-in-your-mouth texture. Remove from the cooker and allow to rest in an empty cooler or Cambro for 1 to 2 hours to redistribute the juices and set the flavors. If you want to serve it hot, go ahead and slice it thinly across the grain. I prefer to wrap and refrigerate overnight and then slice. The pastrami will keep in the refrigerator for up to 5 days.

BRISKET CHILI

Makes about 4 quarts

Nothing beats Old Man Winter down more than a bowl of chili. Brisket freezes very well, and whenever I have leftovers I portion it up in 1-pound plastic freezer bags, label it, and keep it for a time when the weather calls for a nice bowl of chili.

2 pounds red kidney beans,
  soaked in water overnight
1 tablespoon canola oil
1½ cups diced yellow onion
1½ cups diced green bell pepper
1 tablespoon minced garlic
3 quarts water
1 (16-ounce) can tomato sauce
1 (6-ounce) can tomato paste
½ cup light chili powder
1 tablespoon ground cumin
1 teaspoon cayenne
1 teaspoon freshly ground black
  pepper
2 teaspoons granulated garlic
2 teaspoons kosher salt
2 teaspoons sugar
1 teaspoon paprika
2 pounds chopped cooked brisket

Drain and rinse the soaked beans. Heat the oil in a large stockpot over medium heat, add the onion and bell pepper, and cook for 3 minutes. Add the fresh garlic and cook for 2 minutes. Add the beans and water and bring to a boil, then decrease the heat to simmer. Add the tomato sauce and paste, the chili powder, cumin, cayenne, black pepper, granulated garlic, salt, sugar, and paprika and cook for 1 hour or until the beans are tender. Add the brisket and continue to simmer for 30 minutes.

BBQ MEAT LOAF

Serves 4

This is always one of the best sellers in our restaurants. It combines the comfort of homemade meat loaf with a caramelized barbecue sauce for a richer flavor.

2 pounds ground beef

1 tablespoon Ultimate BBQ Rub (page 14)

½ cup Chipotle Bold BBQ Sauce (page 22)

2 tablespoons Worcestershire sauce

2 tablespoons ketchup

⅓ cup diced yellow onion

⅓ cup diced green bell pepper

2 tablespoons panko bread crumbs

½ teaspoon kosher salt

½ teaspoon granulated garlic

½ teaspoon ground black pepper

½ teaspoon seasoned salt

1 large egg

Preheat the oven to 350°F.

In a mixing bowl, combine everything except ¼ cup of the barbecue sauce and mix well. You'll have to get your hands dirty for this one! Fit the mixture into a 9-inch square pan and press down firmly. Cover with a lid or aluminum foil and bake for 1 hour. Remove, drain off excess grease, coat with the remaining ¼ cup of barbecue sauce, and return to the oven for 15 minutes or until the sauce has glazed the meatloaf. Slice and serve.

FLANK STEAK WITH PEPPERS

Serves 4

Do you know what flank steak is? It's beef bacon! No wonder it tastes so good. Flank and skirt steaks are the most popular meats for fajitas. Like chicken wings, they used to be very cheap cuts that have grown in popularity to the point where they now fetch a premium at the meat market. This recipe works well for either, but cut the marinating time in half for the skirt steak, as it is usually a thinner cut.

2 pounds flank steak or skirt steak

⅓ cup lime juice

⅓ cup juice from pickled jalapeños

6 fresh cilantro sprigs, roughly chopped

2 tablespoons Worcestershire sauce

2 tablespoons plus 1 teaspoon Fajita Seasoning (page 16)

1 tablespoon canola oil

1 cup slivered yellow onion

1 cup slivered red bell pepper

1 serrano chile, seeded and diced

1 cup roughly chopped Roma tomato

1 teaspoon minced garlic

1 tablespoon tomato paste

Cooked rice, for serving

Remove the excess fat and silverskin, if any, from the meat. If it came in large pieces, cut into easier-to-grill sizes. Place the steak pieces in a large resealable plastic bag with the lime juice, jalapeño juice, cilantro, Worcestershire, and 1 tablespoon of the fajita seasoning. Shake to coat the steak and then refrigerate for up to 4 hours, turning occasionally.

When ready to cook, prepare a medium-hot grill. Heat the oil in a saucepan over medium heat. Add the onion and peppers and cook for 3 minutes. Add the tomato, garlic, and the 1 teaspoon of fajita seasoning. Cook for 3 minutes, then add the tomato paste. Decrease the heat and allow to simmer slowly while you cook the steak.

Remove the steaks and shake off excess marinade. Season both sides with the remaining 1 tablespoon of fajita seasoning. Place on the grill and cook for 2 to 3 minutes per side or until the internal temperature of the meat registers 130°F. Place on a plate and loosely tent with aluminum foil to rest for 5 minutes. Flank steak, like brisket, needs to be sliced against the grain to be tender. Slice and serve with the sautéed peppers over rice.

THE LAUREN BURGER

Serves 6

My daughter, Lauren, has always been interested in cooking. (I wonder where she got that!) The Southaven Springfest barbecue contest has long hosted the State of Mississippi Youth Cooking Championship, and Lauren, at the ripe old age of six, wanted to enter. This is her recipe, and it won the contest four times!

2 pounds (85/15) ground beef

8 ounces Makin' Bacon (page 66) or your favorite brand, ground

3 tablespoons Worcestershire sauce

2 tablespoons Ultimate BBQ Rub (page 14)

2 teaspoons Grill Seasoning (page 17)

2 tablespoons unsalted butter

6 baby bella (cremini) mushrooms, sliced

1 tablespoon Worcestershire sauce

6 slices provolone cheese

Your favorite buns, dressings, and condiments

Prepare a medium-hot grill. In a large mixing bowl, combine the beef, bacon, Worcestershire, and rub. Mix lightly with your hands to incorporate. Form into 6 patties, then season all sides with the grill seasoning.

Heat a grill to medium-hot. Meanwhile, in a small saucepan over medium heat, melt the butter. Add the mushrooms and sauté for 3 minutes. Add the Worcestershire and decrease the heat to simmer the mushrooms.

Grill the burgers to your desired doneness, about 3 minutes per side for medium. Top with provolone and allow to melt. Place each patty on a bun and top with the mushrooms and your dressings and condiments of choice.

DELTA JUKE BURGERS

Makes 4 double-decker burgers

In the Delta, the local convenience store usually functions as the town grocery, news station, gas station, and restaurant. The menu may be nothing more than sandwiches and a burger, but they are absolutely delicious. When I opened Memphis Barbecue Company, I wanted to re-create the burgers I always ate as a kid while driving around with my grandfather as he made the rounds and caught up on all the goings-on in the area.

JUKE SAUCE

1 cup mayonnaise

2 tablespoons ketchup

1 tablespoon yellow mustard

1½ teaspoons Ultimate BBQ Rub (page 14)

BURGERS

2 pounds (80/20) ground beef

2 tablespoons Grill Seasoning (page 17)

4 slices cheddar cheese

1 yellow onion, sliced crosswise into rounds

4 hamburger buns

Lettuce, tomato slices, and pickles for serving

Preheat a cast-iron skillet or griddle over medium heat.

To make the sauce, combine the mayonnaise, ketchup, mustard, and rub in a small mixing bowl and mix well. Set aside. The sauce can be covered and refrigerated for up to 1 week.

Form the ground beef into eight balls. Flatten slightly, but don't make into patties. Season both sides of the balls with the grill seasoning, then place in the skillet. Using a metal spatula, flatten into thin patties. Sear for 2 minutes or until the patties release from the skillet. Flip and cook for 2 minutes longer for medium. Top every other patty with a slice of cheese and then another patty to make double-deckers. Remove the patties from the skillet and place the onion slices in the skillet to sear for 2 minutes. Place 1½ teaspoons of the juke sauce on the bottom of each bun; dress with lettuce, tomato slices, and pickles; then finish with a slice of seared onion and a set of patties and the top bun.

SPINACH-STUFFED FILET WITH BACON BALSAMIC REDUCTION

Serves 4 to 6

This is a recipe I used to cook quite successfully in contests called "Anything But," meaning anything but competition meats. These contests are usually held on the Friday before the main competition and are mainly a way to show off your cooking skills in a fun event. As we won more contests, we decreased the times we entered the ancillaries, preferring to concentrate on the main event. This is a bit complicated but really makes a showstopper dish.

BACON BALSAMIC REDUCTION

½ cup finely diced Makin' Bacon (page 66) or your favorite brand

1 tablespoon minced garlic

1 cup balsamic vinegar

1 tablespoon honey

BEEF

1 (6-pound) whole beef tenderloin

½ cup plus 1 tablespoon Worcestershire sauce

1 tablespoon unsalted butter

½ cup diced yellow onion

½ cup diced portobello or shiitake mushrooms

1 tablespoon minced garlic

1 teaspoon kosher salt

1 teaspoon freshly ground black pepper

½ teaspoon cayenne

1 pound fresh spinach, stemmed and chopped

1 cup shredded mozzarella cheese

2 tablespoons Grill Seasoning (page 17)

To make the bacon balsamic reduction, place the bacon in a small saucepan over medium heat and cook for 4 minutes. Drain off the grease. Add the garlic and cook for 1 minute, then add the balsamic vinegar and honey, stir, and cook until reduced by half, 4 to 5 minutes. Set aside.

Trim any excess fat and the silverskin from the tenderloin. Remove the "chain," or the thin strip of muscle running down the length of the tenderloin—it has lots of silverskin in it. (I save this and any trimmings to make beef stock.) Remove the "ears," or the large lobes at the top of the tenderloin, and set aside. Cut off the "nose," or 2 inches off the front of the loin, and set aside. Cut off the "tail," or the bottom 4 to 5 inches of the loin, and set aside. You should now have the "trunk," or chateaubriand, of the tenderloin. Except for the chain, the meat trimmings can be used to make filets or tournedos (medallions). Using a very sharp boning knife, start slicing at a 45-degree angle into the trunk and continue to slice it in a spiraling direction (picture a jelly roll) until you have rolled the filet out flat, keeping the meat about ½ inch thick. Place in a resealable plastic bag with the ½ cup of the Worcestershire and seal tightly. Refrigerate for 3 to 4 hours.

Prepare a smoker to cook at 250°F with 3 to 4 chunks of cherry wood. Melt the butter in a skillet, then add the onion and mushrooms and cook until the onion is opaque, 3 to 4 minutes. Add the garlic and cook for 1 minute longer. Add the remaining 1 tablespoon of Worcestershire sauce, the salt, black pepper, and cayenne and cook until the liquid is reduced by half. Add the spinach and cook until wilted, then remove from the heat, add the mozzarella, and stir until the cheese gets slightly melted.

Remove the tenderloin from the refrigerator and place on a cutting board. Spread the filling across the meat to within 1 inch of the sides, then roll up like a jelly roll. Secure by tying butcher's twine around the filet in at least 3 places. Season the outside of the tenderloin with the grill seasoning, then place in the smoker to cook for 2 hours or until the meat registers the desired internal temperature. (I cook it to medium, which is about 145°F.) Remove and allow to rest for 5 minutes, covered, then cut into 1-inch slices. Plate and drizzle with the bacon balsamic reduction.

MARINATED RIBEYES WITH SMOKED VIDALIA ONIONS

Serves 2

When you live, breathe, dream, and plain old obsess about barbecue, there are times when you just don't want to eat it. However, I've never been known to turn down a ribeye! This version has a little kick and will literally melt in your mouth.

2 (14-ounce) ribeye steaks (see Note)
¼ cup Delta Creole Seasoning (page 15)
1 cup canola oil

SMOKED VIDALIA ONIONS

2 medium Vidalia onions
2 tablespoons Worcestershire sauce
2 teaspoons Ultimate BBQ Rub (page 14)
2 tablespoons unsalted butter

The day before you want to cook the ribeyes, season 1 side of each with 1 tablespoon of the Delta Creole Seasoning, then "jaccard" them (see page 5), turn, and repeat with the remaining seasoning. Place both ribeyes in a 1-gallon resealable plastic bag, pour in the oil, and refrigerate overnight.

Trim the ends off each onion and peel off the outer layers. Stand each onion on a trimmed end and, using a paring knife, cut about three-quarters of the way down through each onion. Repeat in a clockwise manner, making the cuts approximately ½-inch apart until you have cut the onions all the way around like spokes on a wagon wheel. Place in a resealable plastic bag, cover with water, and refrigerate overnight.

Remove the steaks from the bag and place on a plate to drain and come up to room temperature.

Prepare a medium-hot grill. Add 1 or 2 chunks of hickory or another bold wood to provide some smoke flavor. Remove the onions from the bag and shake off excess water. Tear off 2 squares of heavy-duty aluminum foil and place around the bottoms (the cut side is the top) of the onions to form a tight bowl. Pour 1 tablespoon of Worcestershire sauce over the top of each onion, sprinkle each with a teaspoon of Ultimate BBQ Rub, and top with a tablespoon of butter. Place on the grill in a medium-heat zone and cook for 20 minutes.

Leave the onions on the grill, add the steaks to the grill, and cook the steaks for 4 to 5 minutes per side, or until the desired temperature is reached. (Aim for an internal temperature of 140°F for medium.) Remove from the grill, loosely tent with aluminum foil, and allow to rest for 5 minutes.

To serve, place the steaks on a plate, remove the onions from the foil, top each steak with an onion, and pour the juices from the foil over the steaks.

NOTE

I typically try to buy high-choice grade or prime (if you can find them) whole ribeyes and cut my own steaks. Ribeyes are the easiest steak to cut—just a little trimming and then cut to the desired thickness. Pack the leftovers well and freeze for later, or cut half into steaks and smoke the other half as a prime rib! An average 14-pound whole ribeye will yield around 14 (¾-inch-thick) steaks after trimming off some fat.

In the competition world, the stars of the show are hogs, ribs, briskets, and butts. However, in the backyard, chicken is by far the most popular. For years I tried to avoid chicken due to "the year of eating chicken" when I was growing up. My grandparents raised chickens, and one year nothing except roosters seemed to hatch. Well, you can't have too many roosters in the henhouse, so we ate a whole lot of chicken. Maybe that's where my fascination with whole hogs and ribeyes started, because it was about 10 years before I even wanted to look at chicken again. Over the years I managed to learn to love chicken and poultry again, and I cook it quite often even outside of competitions.

I have also included some recipes for turkey and, in my opinion, one of the most underrated meats around, quail. My turkey recipe is geared toward the holidays, but I cook turkey year-round and simply adjust the seasonings to fit the season.

6
POULTRY

PERFECT SMOKED CHICKEN

Serves 4 to 6

In the chefy world, there is always a big discussion about how to make perfect roast chicken. While I applaud their efforts, they're slightly off the mark. They should be talking about how to make the perfect smoked chicken. By smoking chicken with a flavorful rub, you elevate an everyday dinner to amazing. I prepare this simply and concentrate on getting a good texture and appearance.

1 (4-pound) whole chicken
3 tablespoons Ultimate BBQ Rub
  (page 14)
½ cup BBQ Mother Sauce
  (page 20)

Prepare a smoker to cook at 250°F with 2 to 3 chunks of apple or cherry wood. (I prefer apple for chicken.)

Using kitchen shears, cut the chicken in half lengthwise and remove excess skin and fat. Sprinkle the rub over both sides of the chicken, then place the chicken in the smoker to cook for 2½ hours, or until the thigh registers 175°F on a meat thermometer. Remove from the smoker and lightly brush with the sauce, then place back in the smoker for 10 minutes to tighten up the sauce. Remove from the smoker and serve.

COMPETITION CHICKEN THIGHS

Makes enough to turn in for a contest, plus some tasters beforehand

Typically, the chicken submitted at a contest really doesn't bear much of a resemblance to chicken you would normally cook in your backyard. The main objectives of contest chicken are to maintain moisture, have "bite-through" skin, and carry the flavor of the sauce. Because of this, most competitors do a type of butter braising. This is a rather complicated recipe, but it works well in competitions, and it'll impress guests.

12 chicken thighs

2 tablespoons Ultimate BBQ Rub
  (page 14)

½ pound (2 sticks) margarine,
  cut into 12 roughly equal pats
  (see Note)

2 cups Sweet Glaze (page 21)

1 cup Memphis-Style Vinegar
  Sauce (page 24)

½ cup honey

On a cutting board, remove the skin from the thighs but do not discard it. Trim any excess fat and meat that are on the ends of the thigh bone. Turn the thigh so the skin side is down and using a paring knife, trim any meat overlapping the bone. Repeat for all thighs.

Place 1 piece of skin on the cutting board with the inside facing up. Using a sharp knife, lightly score the skin in a checkerboard pattern. (I prefer using a santuko knife for this.) Turn the knife so it is at an approximately 20-degree angle and start shaving the fat. The simplest way to do this is to have the edge of the blade facing away from you and hold the skin nearest to you. Rotate the skin until you have shaved off the fat, taking care not to cut through the skin. Yes, this is truly a pain in the you-know-what, but the finished thighs will look great.

Place the thighs bone down in an aluminum pan. Lightly sprinkle the meat with the rub, then tightly wrap a piece of skin back around each thigh. Lightly sprinkle the skins with the rub, then top each thigh with a pat of margarine. Cover and refrigerate overnight.

Prepare a smoker to cook at 250°F using 2 to 3 chunks of cherry wood. Uncover the thighs and place the pan in the smoker for 45 minutes, then cover with heavy-duty aluminum foil and return to the smoker for 45 minutes or until the internal temperature of a thigh registers 165°F.

Mix together the sauces and honey in a small aluminum pan. Remove the thighs from their original pan and set them in the saucepan. Using a spoon, flip sauce over the thighs to coat them. (You really want to avoid brush marks.) Carefully remove the thighs from the sauce by touching the bone ends only and place them back in the original pan. Put the pan back in the smoker for 8 to 10 minutes to make the glaze shiny. Remove and serve.

BUTTERMILK FRIED CHICKEN

Serves 4 to 6

This recipe really speaks from the heart of Mississippi, taking a common item, treating it in a simple yet very flavorful manner, and serving it hot and crispy. For a true Delta rendition, be sure to use a cast-iron skillet. The seasoned flour is my go-to recipe for frying just about anything, and I make it up and keep it in the pantry. Try it on some thin-cut pork chops or Fried Quail with White Gravy (page 104).

MARINADE

2 cups buttermilk

2 cups hot sauce

½ cup Fajita Seasoning (page 16)

1 (4-pound) whole chicken, cut into 8 frying pieces

2 cups canola oil

SEASONED FLOUR

4 cups self-rising flour

½ cup Fajita Seasoning (page 16)

In a large plastic bowl, combine the buttermilk, hot sauce, and fajita seasoning and stir lightly to combine. Add the chicken, coat it thoroughly with the marinade, cover, and refrigerate for 8 to 12 hours, stirring occasionally.

Heat the canola oil in a large cast-iron skillet over medium-high heat to 350°F. An instant-read thermometer is great for checking both the oil temperature and the chicken. Stir together the flour and fajita seasoning on a large plate. One piece at a time, remove the chicken from the marinade, shake off excess liquid, and dredge the chicken in the seasoned flour, making sure all sides are coated.

I typically fry chicken in batches according to the sizes of the different pieces. I cook the breasts and wings together, and the thighs and legs together. Place the breasts in the oil, then 1 minute later add the wings. Cook for at least 3 to 4 minutes before turning, then cook for about 2 minutes longer or until the internal temperature is over 165°F in the breasts. Transfer to a paper towel and start the thighs and legs. Cook for 3 to 4 minutes, then turn and cook for an additional 3 to 4 minutes, or until the internal temperature is 175°F in the thighs. Transfer to a paper-towel-lined plate to drain before serving.

SMOKIN' HOT WINGS

Serves 4 to 6

I like to use whole wings when I'm smoking them, for a simple reason—they don't fall through the grates! These wings have a nice spicy flavor but aren't thermonuclear hot. The smoky and sultry chipotle chile really goes well with barbecue in general, but especially with wings, so I've included two simple sauce options that feature that flavor. You'll need only one, but you could always double the amount of wing ingredients, try both sauces, and have a taste-off.

BBQ WING SAUCE (OPTION 1)

½ cup Chipotle Bold BBQ Sauce
   (page 22)
¼ cup hot sauce
¼ cup honey

SPICY CHIPOTLE
WING GLAZE (OPTION 2)

8 tablespoons (1 stick) unsalted
   butter
½ cup cider vinegar
1½ tablespoons pureed chipotle
   in adobo sauce
2 tablespoons honey
1 tablespoon Dijon mustard
1 tablespoon Ultimate BBQ Rub
   (page 14)

WINGS

2 pounds whole jumbo chicken
   wings
½ cup hot sauce
2 tablespoons Ultimate BBQ Rub
   (page 14)
2 teaspoons cayenne
Ranch or blue cheese dressing,
   for serving

To make the BBQ Wing Sauce, in a small mixing bowl, combine the BBQ sauce, hot sauce, and honey and whisk to incorporate. Set aside.

To make the Spicy Chipotle Wing Glaze, in a small sauté pan over medium heat, melt the butter. Add the vinegar, chipotle, honey, mustard, and rub and whisk to incorporate. Cook until slightly reduced, about 5 minutes, then remove from the heat and set aside.

Rinse the wings and allow to dry. In a large mixing bowl, toss the wings with the hot sauce, rub, and cayenne.

Prepare a smoker to cook at 275°F. For spicy foods, I usually prefer using a couple of chunks of cherry wood as my smoking agent, but just about any wood will do for this recipe.

Place the wings in the smoker and cook for 2 hours or until the skin is crispy and the middle joint will separate from the drummie easily.

Place the wings in a large mixing bowl, add 1 cup of the wing sauce of your choice, and toss until coated. Serve with ranch or blue cheese dressing.

TIP

If you fall into the group that loves to feel their tongue seem to melt down inside their mouth, then simply increase the amount of cayenne pepper or dice up a habanero pepper and mix it in with the sauce while cooking.

HOLIDAY SMOKED TURKEY

Serves up to 8

I'm a traditional girl around the holidays. I want family around, a table set with about four times as much food as we can eat, and in the middle of it all a beautiful smoked turkey. This recipe is brined to add some moisture and flavor. When brining, it is very important to store the turkey where it will maintain proper cool temperatures. If you have a refrigerator that you can place a five-gallon bucket in, that would be perfect. If not, use a cooler just big enough to immerse the bird in the brine with an ice bag. Replace the ice bag every 8 hours or so to keep the temperature cool without adding more water.

BRINE

2 tablespoons chicken base paste
  (See Note, page 111)
4 quarts water
2 cups kosher salt
¾ cup packed light brown sugar
1 tablespoon granulated garlic
1 tablespoon cracked black
  peppercorns
1 tablespoon allspice berries
4 quarts of ice

1 (10- to 12-pound) turkey
Canola oil, for the skin
3 tablespoons Basic BBQ Rub
  (page 13)
1 large onion, quartered
2 large stalks celery, cut into
  4 pieces

Mix the chicken base and water, bring to a boil, and add the salt, brown sugar, granulated garlic, peppercorns, and allspice. Stir until the spices are dissolved. Remove from the heat and allow to cool, then add the ice.

Remove the giblets from inside the turkey and save them for another use if desired. Place the turkey in a cooler or 5-gallon bucket, pour the brine over it, and place a plate on top of the turkey to keep it submerged. Keep cool, either by storing in the refrigerator or by placing ice bags on top and changing them out every few hours. Brine for at least 12 hours and up to 24 hours. The longer it brines, the deeper the flavor will get into the turkey, but it may also increase the saltiness of the meat.

Prepare a smoker to cook at 250°F using 3 to 4 chunks of your favorite fruit wood. I always use apple for turkey. Remove the turkey from the brine, rinse well, then pat dry. Oil the skin of the turkey, then lightly sprinkle the rub over the skin. Place the onion and celery inside the turkey. I fold the wings under themselves to help the turkey sit more evenly.

Place the turkey in the smoker for 2 hours. Remove and wrap with heavy-duty aluminum foil, then return to the smoker. Cook for 2 to 2½ hours longer or until the breast temperature registers 165°F and the thigh temperature 175°F.

NATCHEZ CHICKEN BREASTS

Serves 4

Chicken breasts can get pretty boring, but marination and my zesty vegetable and ham mixture add some flavor and texture to spice up a quick grilled entrée. Natchez, Mississippi, sits slap dab in the middle of the Delta, and with the traditional seasonings and tasso ham in this recipe, I named this dish after the city. I like to serve it with Grilled Corn in the Husk (page 152) and a salad with Balsamic Dressing (page 143) for a nice summer meal.

4 boneless, skinless chicken breasts

1 cup Italian dressing

2 tablespoons olive oil

1 teaspoon minced garlic

1 teaspoon minced shallot

1 yellow onion, slivered

1 red bell pepper, seeded and slivered

6 ounces Tasso Ham (page 60), diced

2 tablespoons Delta Creole Seasoning (page 15)

4 slices provolone cheese

Place the chicken breasts and Italian dressing in a resealable plastic bag, close tightly, and refrigerate for 2 hours. Remove the breasts and shake off excess dressing. Prepare a medium-hot grill.

While the grill is heating, heat the olive oil in a sauté pan over medium heat. Add the garlic and shallot and cook for 1 minute, then add the onion, pepper, and ham and cook for 3 minutes. Decrease the heat to low.

Lightly oil the grates. Season the breasts with the Delta Creole Seasoning and then place them on the grill and cook for 2 minutes. Flip and cook for 2 minutes longer or until done. Using tongs, place a portion of the onion/pepper/ham mixture on top of each breast and then top with cheese. Allow the cheese to melt, then serve.

QUAIL TWO WAYS

Bobwhite quail are truly the bird of the South, and their iconic call always makes me think of my childhood in the country. Bobwhite quail are mainly white meat, delicate and flavorful. Commercially available quail are generally a pharaoh quail breed, with more of a dark meat similar to doves but still delicious. Quail is very delicate, so do not overcook!

FRIED QUAIL WITH WHITE GRAVY

Serves 3 or 4

5 tablespoons bacon grease
¼ cups all-purpose flour
Salt and coarsely ground black pepper
2 cups whole milk, plus milk for dipping
2 cups canola oil
6 quail, butterflied
Seasoned flour (page 99), for coating
Salt and pepper, to taste

Heat the bacon grease in a small saucepan over medium-low heat. Add the flour, ½ teaspoon salt, and 1 teaspoon pepper and start stirring. Keep on stirring. Then stir some more, for about 10 minutes. This is called making a southern roux and is the basis of most gravies and soups in the Delta. As we are making a white gravy, we only need to make a "blond" roux as opposed to a "peanut" or darker roux. Increase the heat to medium, add ½ cup of the milk, and whisk until the gravy gets smooth. Add the remaining 1½ cups milk ½ cup at a time until the milk is incorporated, the gravy is smooth, and the whisk leaves tracks in the gravy as you stir. Taste and add salt and pepper as needed. Keep warm.

In a large skillet, heat the oil to 350°F. Rinse the quail and pat dry. Lightly salt and pepper the quail. Dip the quail in milk, then coat with seasoned flour. Gently lay each quail in the skillet and fry for 2 to 3 minutes, then flip. Cook for 3 minutes longer or until done. Transfer to a paper-towel-lined plate to drain. Plate the quail, top with gravy, and serve.

GRILLED QUAIL WITH BACON BBQ SAUCE

Serves 3 or 4

6 quail, butterflied
2 tablespoons canola oil
2 tablespoons Fajita Seasoning (page 16)
½ cup BBQ Bacon Sauce (page 25), plus sauce for serving

Prepare a medium-hot grill. Rinse the quail and pat dry. Lightly brush each quail with canola oil, then sprinkle lightly with fajita seasoning. Place on the grill skin side down and cook for 4 to 5 minutes, then flip and cook for 4 minutes longer or until done, brushing with BBQ Bacon Sauce in the last 2 minutes. Serve with additional BBQ Bacon Sauce for dipping.

The Delta region was not blessed with an abundance of money, but it made up for that with a wealth of fresh vegetables and seafood either caught locally or brought in from the Gulf of Mexico. These are some of my favorite recipes—some grilled or smoked and some prepared like they would be in a Delta kitchen (well, modified a little!).

7

FISH AND SEAFOOD

FRIED CATFISH WITH TARTAR SAUCE

Serves 2

Mississippi farm-raised catfish is the best in the world. I'm not sure why, but I am sure that the folks in the Delta know their catfish. Farm-raised catfish is clean tasting, with a nice flaky texture when cooked correctly, and will compare favorably to much more expensive fish.

TARTAR SAUCE

1 cup mayonnaise

2 tablespoons sweet pickle relish

1 tablespoon finely diced yellow onion

1½ teaspoons lemon juice

Pinch of kosher salt

Pinch of coarsely ground black pepper

CATFISH

Canola oil, for frying

2 cups self-rising yellow cornmeal

1 tablespoon coarsely ground black pepper

1½ tablespoons kosher salt

1 teaspoon granulated garlic

1 teaspoon onion powder

4 catfish fillets

1 cup buttermilk

Slices of yellow onion or scallions for serving (optional)

To make the tartar sauce, combine all the ingredients in a small mixing bowl, whisk well, then set aside.

Heat 2 inches of oil in a large skillet or a deep fryer to 350°F. Combine the cornmeal, pepper, salt, granulated garlic, and onion powder on a large plate and mix well. Rinse the fillets, then lightly dust them with the seasoned cornmeal. Dredge through the buttermilk, then lay one side in the cornmeal mixture and press lightly to make sure the cornmeal sticks. Flip and press the other side. Gently lay each fillet in the hot oil and cook for 2 to 3 minutes, then flip and cook for 2 to 3 minutes longer, or until the coating is crunchy and the fish is cooked thoroughly. Remove the fillets and drain on paper towels, then serve with the tartar sauce on the side. In Mississippi, it's also traditional to serve catfish with a slice of yellow onion or a whole scallion.

BBQ SHRIMP *and* GRITS

Serves 4

"BBQ Shrimp" is kind of a misnomer. It's not really grilled or smoked, but rather sautéed in barbecue seasonings and butter. The New Orleans tradition is to use whole, head-on shrimp and get the barbecue flavors by peeling the shrimp while dining and transferring the seasonings in the sauce to the shrimp from your fingers—very messy! I prefer to peel the shrimp and then use the flavorful butter and bacon sauce to help jazz up the grits as well. I like to serve this with my Balsamic Grilled Vegetables (page 141).

1 pound 21–25 count shrimp
   (preferably gulf shrimp)
8 ounces Makin' Bacon (page 66)
   or your favorite brand, diced
3 tablespoons unsalted butter
2 tablespoons Basic BBQ Rub
   (page 13)
Prepared grits (recipe follows)

Peel and devein the shrimp, leaving the tails intact (see Note).

Heat a skillet over medium heat, add the bacon pieces, and cook until lightly crispy, about 3 minutes. Transfer the bacon to a paper-towel-lined plate and drain off all but about 1 tablespoon of the grease. Add the shrimp to the skillet and cook for 2 minutes, then flip and cook for 1 minute longer. Return the bacon to the pan, then add the butter. After the butter melts, sprinkle on the rub and allow to dissolve, about 1 minute.

To serve, place some grits on each plate, then top with about 6 shrimp per person. Pour about a tablespoon of the butter sauce over the top and serve.

NOTE

You can save the shells to make homemade shrimp stock for Shrimp Gumbo (page 122) or other dishes.

GRITS

Serves 4

There is absolutely no comparison between real grits and that pale, insipid dish served at most breakfast places. We buy our grits wholesale from The Original Grit Girl in Oxford, Mississippi, where Georgeanne Ross stone-grinds the grits every week. If you can't score any of her wonderful grits, choose another brand that makes a more traditional, preferably stone-ground, grit. This recipe is made for our BBQ Shrimp and Grits.

3 cups water
1 cup dry stone-ground grits
1½ teaspoons chicken base paste
  (see Note, page 133)
½ cup heavy cream
½ teaspoon kosher salt
½ teaspoon white pepper

Place 1½ cups of the water in a stockpot, then add the grits, chicken base, cream, salt, and pepper. Bring to a boil, then decrease the heat and simmer for 25 to 30 minutes, stirring frequently to keep the grits from sticking and adding more water as the grits thicken.

TSUNAMI SHRIMP

Serves 4 to 6

I used this recipe to win the One Bite Challenge at a Kingsford Invitational. It's very simple and can be prepared mostly in advance and then cooked quickly. It makes a great hors d'oeuvre.

1 pound 21–25 count shrimp

1 pound Makin' Bacon strips, preferably peppered bacon (page 66), or your favorite brand

½ cup finely diced pickled jalapeños

½ (8-ounce) package cream cheese

½ cup Thai sweet chili sauce

Peel the shrimp, leaving the tails intact (see Note). Using a small knife, slice down the center of shrimp (to form a pocket for the cream cheese mixture later) and devein.

Slice each bacon strip in half. Place the bacon in a skillet and cook over medium heat until the bacon is beginning to render its fat but is not browned. Set aside to cool.

Prepare a medium-hot grill with the coals to one side. Place the jalapeños in a small mixing bowl with the cream cheese and use a fork to stir until well blended. Take each shrimp and, using a fork, place about 1½ teaspoons of the cream cheese mixture in the pocket where the shrimp was sliced. Fold the shrimp around the cream cheese mixture, then wrap with a half strip of bacon and secure with a toothpick.

Place the shrimp on the grill so the tails are away from the hottest part. Cook for 2 to 3 minutes, turning as needed, or until the bacon is crisped and the shrimp are done. In the last minute of cooking, brush each side with the chili sauce. The bacon will render fat and cause flame-ups, so be prepared to move the shrimp to the cooler part of the grill as needed. This is not a "set it and forget it" recipe! Remove from the grill and serve with additional chili sauce for dipping.

NOTE

You can save the shells to make homemade shrimp stock for Shrimp Gumbo (page 122) or other dishes.

BRONZED CRAPPIE
WITH WATERMELON SALSA

Serves 3 or 4

Crappie is one of the most prized fish in the South for its beautiful white, flaky texture. It is normally fried, but I love to bring a little different flavor occasionally. This recipe works well for just about any fish, so try it with your favorite. I love to prepare this in a skillet on the grill, which will give it that little hint of smoke that makes all the difference. And since summertime brings a wealth of watermelons to Mississippi, this salsa brings together cooling watermelon with what is basically a pico de gallo for a refreshing flavor.

WATERMELON SALSA

1 cup diced tomato, preferable heirloom

1 cup diced seeded (or seedless) watermelon, seeds removed

½ cup diced yellow onion

¼ cup finely diced jalapeño

Leaves from about 10 fresh cilantro sprigs, chopped

1 tablespoon canola oil

2 teaspoons kosher salt

1 teaspoon coarsely ground black pepper

1½ teaspoons granulated garlic

FISH

4 tablespoons (½ stick) margarine, melted

¼ cup Delta Creole Seasoning (page 15)

1 pound crappie fillets

Cooked white rice, for serving

To make the salsa, place the tomato and watermelon in a colander for 5 minutes to drain excess liquid. Transfer to a mixing bowl, add the onion, jalapeño, cilantro, oil, salt, pepper, and granulated garlic, and stir well. Refrigerate until ready to serve.

Prepare a grill with charcoal and 1 to 2 chunks of wood. For fish, I like apple wood, but any mild wood will do. We're just looking for a hint of smoke. Place a skillet or griddle pan on the grill and allow it to heat.

Place the melted margarine in a saucer. Add the Delta Creole Seasoning and mix with a fork. Dredge the crappie fillets through the mixture to coat. Lay the fillets in the preheated pan on the grill and cook for 2 minutes, or until the fillets release easily from the pan. Flip and cook for 1 to 2 minutes longer, depending on the thickness of the fillets. Crappie fillets are usually thin, so you may need to adjust the cooking times for other types of fish.

Serve on a bed of rice and top with watermelon salsa.

FRIED OYSTERS WITH RED PEPPER MAYO

Serves 4 to 6

My grandfather was a true gentleman, and because fried oysters were his favorite meal, they will always hold a special place in my heart. I remember having dinner with him and listening to his stories and enjoying a big plate of homemade fried oysters.

Scratch-made mayonnaise is very easy and so delicious. I love to add my own accent flavors. Here I use roasted red peppers, but you can easily make it with chipotle peppers, herbs, or really any flavor you like. You can also substitute for the vinegar—champagne vinegar, white wine vinegar, or even herb vinegar.

To save time, I roast red peppers when I'm grilling another meal, cut them into strips, then pack them in small jars with olive oil. They will keep in the refrigerator for up to 2 weeks.

RED PEPPER MAYO

1 large egg yolk

1 teaspoon minced garlic

½ teaspoon salt

1 tablespoon Dijon mustard

1 teaspoon lemon juice

1 tablespoon red wine vinegar

½ cup chopped roasted red pepper

½ cup extra virgin olive oil (I use the lightest flavor I can find)

½ cup canola oil

FRIED OYSTERS

3 cups canola oil

1 cup self-rising flour

1 tablespoon salt

1½ teaspoons freshly ground black pepper

1 cup self-rising yellow cornmeal

24 fresh oysters, shucked

2 cups milk

Make the red pepper mayo: In a nonreactive bowl, whisk together the egg yolk, garlic, salt, and mustard. Whisk in the lemon juice and vinegar, then add the red pepper. Using a small immersion blender on low speed, drizzle in the oils until an emulsion forms. Cover and refrigerate until ready to serve. If you don't have an immersion blender, you can use a whisk or a regular blender on low speed.

In a skillet, heat the oil to 350°F. In a shallow dish, combine the flour, salt, pepper, and cornmeal. Dunk the oysters in milk, then drop them into the cornmeal mixture and toss to bread. Transfer the breaded oysters to another plate until all are breaded. Carefully place the oysters in the hot oil and fry for 3 minutes or until crisp. Use a slotted spoon or tongs to remove the oysters and place them on a paper-towel-lined plate to drain. Serve with red pepper mayo.

BBQ OYSTERS

Serves 2 to 3

This dish is one of my favorite ways to serve oysters. It makes a really fun appetizer to share while hanging out at the grill. The fire gives them just a hint of smoke that really complements the seasoning.

8 tablespoons (1 stick) unsalted butter

2 tablespoons Ultimate BBQ Rub (page 14)

1 teaspoon dried rosemary

12 fresh oysters on the half shell

Prepare a medium-hot grill. In a small saucepan over medium-low heat, melt the butter, then add the rub and rosemary and stir to form a thin paste. Using a spoon, drizzle each oyster with about 1 teaspoon of the butter sauce, then place on the grill over a hot area—flames licking around the shells will help the flavor! Cook for 3 to 4 minutes or until the oysters are hot but not overcooked.

GINGER SALMON WITH PINEAPPLE CHIPOTLE GLAZE

Serves 4

Yes, I understand that this isn't very Delta, but it tastes so good I just had to include it. This marinade and glaze will work for any firm-bodied fish or even chicken or steak—it's very versatile. I am under standing orders to deliver extras of this to my mom whenever I make it, but sometimes I just don't tell her so I can keep it. Extra glaze will keep in the fridge for up to 2 weeks.

1 cup soy sauce

½ cup pineapple juice

1 cup packed light brown sugar

½ cup canola oil

1 tablespoon coarsely ground black pepper

1 tablespoon granulated garlic

2 tablespoons chopped fresh ginger

4 (8-ounce) skinless salmon fillets

PINEAPPLE CHIPOTLE GLAZE

2 tablespoons pureed chipotle chiles in adobo sauce

1 cup apple cider vinegar

½ cup pineapple juice

½ cup soy sauce

4 cups granulated sugar

In a nonreactive container, combine the 1 cup of soy sauce, ½ cup of pineapple juice, brown sugar, oil, pepper, granulated garlic, and ginger and mix well. Add the salmon fillets. Cover and refrigerate for 8 to 12 hours, turning occasionally.

To make the glaze, place the chiles and a splash of the vinegar in a blender and blend until smooth. Place the pineapple juice in a large stockpot over medium heat and cook until slightly reduced, about 2 minutes. Add the chipotle mixture and cook for 3 minutes. Add the soy sauce, granulated sugar, and remaining vinegar and bring to a boil. Decrease the heat and cook for 10 minutes. This recipe boils quickly, so stir constantly. The glaze should lightly coat the back of a spoon when done. Remove from the heat and let cool. The glaze can be made ahead and refrigerated overnight.

Prepare a medium-hot grill and lightly oil the grates. Remove the salmon from the marinade and shake off excess liquid. Place on the grill for 3 to 4 minutes, then turn and cook for 3 to 4 minutes longer, depending upon the thickness of the fillets. In the last minute of cooking, liberally brush on the glaze and allow to thicken slightly. Serve with additional glaze on the side if desired.

PO'BOYS WITH RÉMOULADE SAUCE

Serves 3 or 4

Po'boys are basically a sandwich on a French loaf. You can pretty much put anything in a nice crusty loaf of bread and call it a po'boy, but traditionally it's made with fried oysters, crawfish, or shrimp.

RÉMOULADE SAUCE

2 cups mayonnaise

2 tablespoons finely diced scallion

1 tablespoon finely diced yellow onion

1½ tablespoons finely diced celery

2 tablespoons Worcestershire sauce

1 tablespoon whole-grain mustard

1 tablespoon ketchup

1½ teaspoons prepared horseradish

1 teaspoon dry mustard

1 teaspoon kosher salt

SANDWICHES

French loaves, cut into 6-inch pieces

Shredded lettuce

Tomato slices

Sliced pickles

Fried Oysters (page 116), Fried Crawfish (recipe follows), or BBQ Shrimp (page 110)

To make the rémoulade sauce, mix all the ingredients together in a bowl and store in the refrigerator until ready to serve. The sauce will keep, covered, for up to 5 days.

To build the po'boys, slice each 6-inch piece of French bread in half but not all the way through. Add a thick slathering of rémoulade, then top with lettuce, sliced tomato, pickles, and your favorite seafood.

FRIED CRAWFISH

Serves 3 or 4

Crawfish season signals spring in the Delta, and you will see many roadside stands serving spicy boiled crawfish. Crawfish tails are an even greater delicacy. If you've ever been to a crawfish boil, you know what a pain it is to get the tails! Luckily, today you can buy a decent-quality frozen crawfish tail at most supermarkets. These fried tails make a great appetizer (known around the Delta as "Cajun popcorn") with rémoulade sauce (page 120) for dipping.

3 cups canola oil

2 cups self-rising flour

¼ cup Delta Creole Seasoning (page 15), plus more for serving

2 cups milk

1 pound crawfish tails

In a skillet, heat the oil to 350°F. Place the flour in a shallow dish and mix the seasoning into it. Place the milk in a bowl.

The best tool for dipping crawfish tails is a small, fine-mesh skimmer. Place a few tails in the skimmer, dip into the milk, shake off excess, and place in the flour. Toss to coat, then shake off excess flour. Bread the remaining tails. Place the tails in the skillet and cook for 3 to 4 minutes or until hot and crispy. Remove and drain on a paper-towel-lined plate. Lightly sprinkle with more Delta Creole Seasoning and serve hot.

SHRIMP GUMBO

Makes about 1 gallon

I love shrimp gumbo, though being from Mississippi I am partial to okra gumbos, rather than filé gumbos. This recipe is one that will make you hungry all day as the wonderful aromas circulate through your kitchen. Whenever you cook shrimp at home, save the shells and freeze them until you can save up enough to make a stock. Homemade shrimp stock is the key to this dish!

8 tablespoons (1 stick) unsalted butter

¾ cup all-purpose flour

2 pounds andouille sausage

1 cup slivered yellow onion

½ cup chopped green bell pepper

½ cup chopped celery

1 tablespoon minced garlic

1 tablespoon tomato paste

1 pound sliced okra

3 quarts Shrimp Stock (recipe follows)

1 (12-ounce) bottle dark beer

1 tablespoon Worcestershire sauce

2 bay leaves

1 teaspoon dried thyme

1 teaspoon freshly ground black pepper

2 teaspoons kosher salt

1 tablespoon Delta Creole Seasoning (page 15)

2 pounds 40–50 count shrimp, peeled and deveined

8 ounces crawfish tails (optional)

Cooked white rice for serving

Melt the butter in a heavy skillet over medium heat. Start whisking in the flour a tablespoon or two at a time until all the flour is incorporated. Continue to whisk constantly until the roux develops a nutty aroma and darkens to the color of peanut butter, 20 to 25 minutes. You may continue to cook it until it becomes very dark, as long as you're willing to whisk it for up to 45 minutes! Remove from the heat and set aside.

Brown the andouille sausage in a large stockpot over medium heat. Remove the sausage from the pot, leaving about 2 tablespoons of the rendered fat in the pot. Add the onion, pepper, and celery to the pot and cook until soft, about 10 minutes. Add the garlic and cook until golden, about 2 minutes. Add the tomato paste, stir, then add the okra and cook for 3 minutes. Return the sausage to the pot and stir in the shrimp stock, beer, Worcestershire, bay leaves, thyme, black pepper, salt, and Delta Creole Seasoning. Bring to a boil, then decrease the heat to simmer. Add the shrimp and crawfish tails and cook for 5 minutes or until the shrimp is done. While stirring, slowly add ¾ cup of the roux and mix until incorporated. Check the consistency and, if you like more body, add the remaining roux. (If you don't use all of the roux, cover and refrigerate any remaining for up to 2 weeks). Remove and discard the bay leaves, then serve hot over white rice.

SHRIMP STOCK

Makes 3 quarts

8 cups lightly packed shrimp shells
1 cup dry white wine
1 gallon water
1 cup coarsely chopped onion
3 stalks celery, coarsely chopped
4 cloves garlic, crushed
2 bay leaves
1 tablespoon black peppercorns
½ teaspoon dried thyme

Heat a large stockpot over medium heat and place the shrimp shells in the pot. Cook for 4 minutes, stirring often. Deglaze the pan with the white wine, then add the water, onion, celery, garlic, bay leaves, peppercorns, and thyme and bring to a boil. Decrease the heat and simmer for 45 minutes. Strain the stock before using.

Go to most houses in the Delta, and the sides will be the stars of the show. Many times, the bounty of the land was available, but not necessarily a lot of meat. So Delta cooks augmented meals with lots of sides, flavorful condiments, and the freshest vegetables available.

I believe in versatility when cooking, a tradition well practiced in my home state. The flavors you show in your food should be an expression of you and your family, and I'm a firm believer in using recipes as a guide, not a map. Most of these recipes, just like those in other chapters, are open to interpretation. If you like to accent a certain ingredient, add an extra pinch! That's the true heritage of the Delta—taking common dishes and making them uncommonly good.

8
SIDES
AND
SUCH

SUNDAY POTATO SALAD

Serves 4 to 6

Mention potato salad anywhere in the South, and you'll start a fight just about as quickly as if you talk about how much better your barbecue is than your neighbor's. All southerners think the way their mama made potato salad is the only way to make it. Well, I don't know your mama, but if she had tried this recipe you would have grown up eating it this way! I like to leave the skin on, but it's perfectly acceptable to peel the potatoes if you want.

RANCH SEASONING MIX

¼ cup dried buttermilk

1 teaspoon dried dill

¼ teaspoon white pepper

1½ teaspoons dried parsley

1 teaspoon onion powder

1 teaspoon kosher salt

½ teaspoon garlic powder

SALAD

2 pounds red potatoes, peeled or not, cut into eighths

1 cup sour cream

1 cup mayonnaise

½ cup milk

1 bunch scallions, green parts only, diced

1 cup chopped crisp-cooked bacon, from about ½ pound Makin' Bacon (page 66) or your favorite brand

Combine all the ingredients for the ranch seasoning mix in a small mixing bowl and whisk to blend.

Place the potatoes on a cutting board, then cut in half. Cut each half into four pieces, trying to keep the sizes as uniform as possible. Place the potato pieces in a large stockpot with water to cover, bring to a boil, and cook until soft but not mushy, about 10 minutes. Remove and drain. Allow to cool to room temperature, then place in large bowl. Add the sour cream, mayonnaise, milk, scallions, bacon bits, and seasoning mix and fold with a spatula until well mixed. Refrigerate for at least 2 hours before serving.

NOTE

Add 2 tablespoons of the seasoning mix to 1 cup of mayonnaise and ½ cup of buttermilk to make a great ranch dressing!

COLESLAW

Serves 6 to 8

No side is as ubiquitous at a barbecue party as coleslaw. They just go together. Coleslaw in the South is kind of personal, and we get more comments about it in the restaurants than about any other item. People typically love coleslaw that their mama made, and they get pretty upset about being served other types. Well, this slaw is how my mother made it (with my own little twist), and that's the last thing I'll say about that!

1 medium head green cabbage
1 cup shredded carrot (about 2 medium)

DRESSING

1 cup mayonnaise
1½ teaspoons yellow mustard
¼ cup sugar
¼ cup white vinegar
½ teaspoon coarsely ground black pepper
¼ teaspoon salt
Pinch of ground cumin
Pinch of chipotle chile powder

Quarter the cabbage, slice out the core, then make thin cuts down the face of each piece of cabbage. You can give it a couple more chops if you want less length to the pieces. Place the cabbage in a large bowl and toss with the shredded carrot.

In a medium mixing bowl, combine all the dressing ingredients and stir well to mix. Add 1 to 1½ cups of dressing to the cabbage mixture and toss to coat. The slaw should look moist, but not too wet, as coleslaw will weep after it sits.

GRAPE SALAD

Serves 6 to 8

At the risk of being a little macabre, a whole lot of recipes make it through the South by being passed around at funerals. It's a tradition to make a dish and bring it to the home of the bereaved, and of course, when the third cousin makes a delicious item, everyone else has to get the recipe. That's how I got this recipe, and it is my husband's favorite thing to have at Thanksgiving dinner.

1 cup sour cream

1 (8-ounce) package cream cheese, softened

½ cup granulated sugar

1 teaspoon vanilla extract

2 pounds seedless green grapes, rinsed

2 pounds seedless red grapes, rinsed

1 cup packed light brown sugar

1½ cups pecan halves

In a large mixing bowl, mix together the sour cream, cream cheese, granulated sugar, and vanilla until well blended. Fold in the grapes, then pour the salad into a nice serving bowl. Sprinkle with the brown sugar, then arrange the pecan halves over the top. Cover and chill for at least 2 hours before serving.

BAKED BBQ BEANS

Serves 4 to 6

Yes, I have been known to cheat on baked beans and just "doctor" up some canned ones, but when I'm in a make-it-from-scratch mode, this recipe really fits the bill. I generally don't put pulled pork in my beans, but feel free to toss some in if the mood hits you.

1 pound dried navy beans, soaked in water overnight, drained, and rinsed

2 teaspoons kosher salt

6 cups water

½ cup trimmings from Makin' Bacon (page 66) or your favorite brand, diced

¼ cup diced celery

1 large yellow onion, diced

1 green bell pepper, seeded and diced

1 red bell pepper, seeded and diced

1½ teaspoons minced garlic

1 cup BBQ Mother Sauce (page 20)

⅓ cup molasses

¼ cup yellow mustard

2 tablespoons cider vinegar

⅓ cup packed light brown sugar

½ cup Ultimate BBQ Rub (page 14)

1 teaspoon cayenne

Combine the beans, salt, and water in a large pot, bring to a boil, and then decrease the heat and simmer for 3 to 3½ hours or until the beans are soft.

Preheat the oven to 350°F. In a small saucepan over medium heat, cook the bacon trimmings for 3 to 4 minutes, then add the celery, onion, and peppers and cook for 3 to 4 minutes, until tender. Add the garlic and cook for 1 more minute. In a large casserole dish, combine the beans, the bacon and pepper mixture, the mother sauce, molasses, mustard, vinegar, brown sugar, rub, and cayenne and stir. Cover and bake for 1 hour, then uncover and continue to bake until thick and bubbly, 15 to 20 minutes longer.

RED BEANS *and* RICE

Serves 6 to 8

Red beans and rice is a New Orleans dish traditionally served on Mondays, when cooks would put on a big pot of red beans to simmer while they attended to the weekly wash. The tradition stuck, as many restaurants in the region serve "RB&R" as a Monday special to this day. This version will happily light a small signal fire on your palate to keep you wanting another bite. I love to serve it with a nice piece of seared smoked sausage on the side.

1 tablespoon canola oil

2 pounds smoked sausage, cut into half-moons

1 green bell pepper, seeded and slivered

1 red bell pepper, seeded and slivered

1 medium onion, slivered

1 medium stalk celery, diced

2 tablespoons minced garlic

1 pound Tasso Ham (page 60), diced (optional)

2 bay leaves

1 tablespoon kosher salt

1 tablespoon black pepper

1 tablespoon Delta Creole Seasoning (page 15)

2 tablespoons chicken base paste (see Note)

1 tablespoon ham base paste (see Note)

6 quarts water

3 pounds dried small red beans, soaked in water overnight, drained, and rinsed

Cooked rice for serving

Heat the oil in large stockpot over medium-high heat. Drop in the sausage and sear it, about 3 minutes, then remove it from the pot but leave the oil. Add the peppers, onion, and celery and cook for 3 minutes or until the vegetables are softened. Add the garlic, tasso ham, bay leaves, salt, black pepper, and Delta Creole Seasoning and cook for 2 minutes. Add the chicken base, ham base, water, and beans and bring to a boil. Decrease the heat and simmer for 2 to 3 hours or until the beans are softened and the soup starts taking on some body, where all the ingredients begin to incorporate. If you want it a little thicker, mash about 20 percent of the beans against the side of the pot and stir into the stew. Serve over rice.

NOTE

I like Minor's brand bases as they are high quality and less salty than other brands we've tried. In place of the pastes and the 6 quarts of water, you could use ½ gallon of chicken stock and ½ gallon of pork stock along with 2 quarts of water.

TURNIP GREENS

Serves 4 to 6

This procedure works well for just about any type of greens, but turnip greens are my favorite. Serve with some Cast-Iron Corn Bread (page 151), Pinto Beans (page 140), and Sweet Pepper Sauce (page 137), and, really, that's all you need!

4 to 5 pounds turnip greens

2 cups water, plus water for braising the greens

1 tablespoon canola oil

1 pound trimmings from Makin' Bacon (page 66) or your favorite brand, diced

1 yellow onion, finely chopped

1 teaspoon sugar

½ teaspoon freshly ground black pepper

Salt

Cut the stems off the turnip greens and discard. Rinse the leaves well. Place in a large stockpot, cover with water, and bring to a simmer over medium heat. Drain and set aside, then rinse out the pot. Add the canola oil to the pot along with the bacon trimmings and onion. Cook until the bacon is slightly rendered, about 4 minutes, then add the greens and the 2 cups of water. Bring to a boil, then decrease the heat, cover, and simmer for 45 to 60 minutes or until the greens are tender. Season with the sugar, pepper, and salt and serve.

SMOKED TOMATO BISQUE

Serves 2 or 3

Tomato soup is a classic comfort soup that goes great with a grilled cheese sandwich. I like to smoke the tomatoes for an extra layer of flavor.

SMOKED TOMATOES

5 medium tomatoes, cored and cut in half
1 tablespoon olive oil
1 tablespoon minced garlic
1 teaspoon kosher salt
Finely ground black pepper

SOUP

1 tablespoon olive oil
1 medium onion, finely chopped
½ cup shredded carrot
2½ cups chicken stock
1 tablespoon tomato paste
⅔ cup heavy cream
5 to 6 fresh basil leaves, slivered
½ teaspoon white pepper
½ cup croutons

Prepare a smoker to cook at 250°F. Place the tomatoes cut side down in a small aluminum pan, drizzle with the olive oil, and sprinkle with the garlic, salt, and pepper. Place in the smoker and cook for 2 hours, then remove and set aside.

To make the soup, heat the olive oil in a large stockpot over medium heat, then add the onion and carrot and cook for 4 to 5 minutes, until the onion is opaque. Scrape the tomatoes into the pot, add the chicken stock, and cook for 20 to 30 minutes or until the tomatoes are soft. Add the tomato paste and stir, then use an immersion blender to puree for 20 seconds. Add the cream, basil, and pepper and puree until smooth. Taste and adjust the seasonings. Ladle into bowls and serve with a few croutons sprinkled on top.

NOTES

If you adjust the ingredient amounts to make more or less sauce, use a 3:1 ratio of water to cider to make enough liquid to slightly cover any amount you make.

If cowhorn peppers aren't available, feel free to substitute your choice of peppers according to the heat level you're looking for—Anaheims, sweet peppers, serranos; really, the choices are endless!

SWEET PEPPER SAUCE

Makes 4 cups

This is the condiment of choice for pinto beans, turnip greens, peas—heck, dang near anything! This is my grandmother's recipe, but you can use this method and change the flavor very easily. Like more spice? Add a few serranos or jalapeños. Want a more savory vinegar flavor? Cut down the sugar and add some whole garlic cloves and peppercorns. One note: Make this when the kids are at school, as the vinegar smell will clear the house!

1 cup cider vinegar

3 cups water (see Notes)

1 teaspoon kosher salt

2 cups sugar

1 pound green and red cowhorn peppers (see Notes)

In a large stockpot, combine the vinegar, water, salt, and sugar, stir well, and bring to a boil, then reduce the heat and allow the mixture to reduce by one-fourth. Rinse the peppers and place them in the pot. The liquid should just cover the peppers. Continue to boil for 7 to 8 minutes or until the peppers begin to slightly lose their color. Remove from the heat, pull out the peppers, and arrange them in jars. Fill the jars with liquid and seal tightly. Let the jars cool to room temperature, then refrigerate until ready to use. They'll keep for up to 2 weeks. If you're a canner, you can process the jars according to your canning equipment manufacturer's recommendations for other pepper sauces.

MACARONI *and* CHEESE

Serves 4 to 6

In the South, we don't make baked lobster mac and cheese with a Gruyère crust; we make macaroni in a rich, creamy cheese sauce and are dang happy to have it!

2 cups elbow macaroni
4 cups water
1 tablespoon olive oil
4 tablespoons (½ stick) unsalted
  butter
¼ cup all-purpose flour
2 cups whole milk
½ teaspoon salt
½ teaspoon ground black pepper
2 cups shredded American cheese
1 cup shredded cheddar cheese

Cook the macaroni in the water and oil according to the package directions. Drain, transfer to a bowl, and set aside.

Melt the butter in a medium saucepan over medium heat, then stir in the flour and cook for 2 minutes, stirring occasionally. Whisk in the milk, salt, and pepper and cook until slightly thickened, about 2 minutes. Add the cheeses about a cup at a time, stirring until melted after each addition. Pour the cheese sauce into the cooked macaroni and stir. Taste, add more salt and pepper if needed, and serve.

PINTO BEANS

Serves 4 to 6

Every so often I get a craving for home cooking and make a pot of pintos, a mess of greens, some corn bread, mashed potatoes, and a fried pork chop. Lord, let that be my last meal! Pintos are easy to cook and will simmer away happily for hours while you prepare other things. I cook them very simply. If you would like to add tomatoes, green peppers, or whatnot, feel free—pintos are very forgiving.

1 tablespoon canola oil or bacon grease

½ cup diced Makin' Bacon (page 66) or your favorite brand or salt pork

1 pound dried pinto beans, soaked in water overnight, drained, and rinsed

1 teaspoon salt

1 teaspoon sugar

Heat the oil in a large stockpot over medium-high heat. When the oil is hot, add the bacon and cook for 2 minutes. Add the beans and cover with water. Bring to a boil, then decrease the heat to simmer, stir in the salt and sugar, and cook for 2 to 3 hours or until tender.

BALSAMIC GRILLED VEGETABLES

Serves 4

I really love to grill summer vegetables, and I typically have them at any meal I'm grilling. Just cut some vegetables into evenly sized pieces, toss lightly with oil and salt and pepper, grill, and you've got a great side. This dish marinates the vegetables in balsamic dressing and then gives the vegetables a flavor that goes well with just about any entrée.

1 pound asparagus

1 red onion

1 red bell pepper

2 large portobello mushrooms, stems removed

1 cup Balsamic Dressing (page 143)

Trim the bottom, tough areas from the asparagus. Peel the onion, cut it in half, then cut it crosswise into narrow strips. Stem and seed the red bell pepper, then cut it into narrow strips as well. Cut the mushroom caps into ½-inch strips. Place all of the vegetables in a nonreactive container (I love resealable plastic bags for this) and add the dressing. Marinate for 2 hours, turning the bag after 1 hour.

Prepare a medium-hot grill. Remove the vegetables from the bag and shake off excess dressing. Place on a grilling rack or screen on the grate and cook for 4 to 5 minutes, turning as needed. I like to get a little char on the asparagus while maintaining some crispness.

BALSAMIC DRESSING

Makes 2 ¼ cups

Balsamic dressing is one of my favorites. I keep some in my refrigerator at all times. It's very versatile and works well both as a salad dressing and as a marinade.

½ teaspoon minced garlic
1½ teaspoons Dijon mustard
¼ cup balsamic vinegar
1 tablespoon red wine vinegar
1 tablespoon honey
½ teaspoon kosher salt
¼ teaspoon coarsely ground black pepper
⅓ cup olive oil
1½ cups canola oil

Place the garlic, mustard, vinegars, honey, salt, and pepper in a mixing bowl and stir to mix. Combine the oils in a large measuring cup. Insert an immersion blender into the mixing bowl and turn it on low. While mixing, slowly drizzle the oil blend into the mixing bowl to form an emulsion. If you don't have an immersion blender, you can use a whisk or a regular blender on low speed. The dressing will keep, covered, in the refrigerator for up to 5 days. You may need to leave it at room temperature for a little while and recombine the ingredients before using.

FRIED CABBAGE

Serves 4 to 6

I was experimenting in the kitchen one day and worked out this recipe. It's very simple to make but has a unique flavor.

1 medium head green cabbage
2 tablespoons canola oil
2 tablespoons Fajita Seasoning
   (page 16)

Quarter the cabbage and cut out the core. Turn one quarter on its side and slice thinly down the face to shred it, then roughly chop the shreds. Repeat with the remaining quarters. Heat the oil in a large skillet over medium-high heat and add the cabbage and fajita seasoning. Cook over medium-high heat for 5 to 6 minutes or until wilted and golden.

CORN CASSEROLE

Serves 4 to 6

This can be made with frozen or canned corn, but use fresh sweet corn for a really rich taste. The difference between whole-kernel corn and cream-style corn is how you cut it from the ear. For whole-kernel, cut at the base of the kernel. For cream-style, cut halfway through the kernel, then turn your knife over and scrape the remaining kernels to extract the milk.

1 cup fresh whole-kernel corn
1 cup fresh cream-style corn
1 cup sour cream
⅔ cup all-purpose flour
½ cup yellow cornmeal
3 tablespoons sugar
1 tablespoon baking powder
¼ teaspoon salt
½ cup melted unsalted butter
1 cup shredded cheddar cheese

Preheat the oven to 350°F and grease a 9 by 13-inch baking dish. In a large bowl, combine all of the ingredients and mix well. Pour into the prepared pan and bake for 45 minutes, until golden and bubbly.

CUCUMBER SALAD

Makes 8 cups

This is a basically a quick pickle, but it retains more of a fresh cucumber taste than processed pickles. The freshness makes it a great side for barbecue.

6 cups sliced cucumber
1 cup slivered onion
1 cup slivered green bell pepper
1 teaspoon salt
1 cup white vinegar
2 cups sugar
1 teaspoon celery seeds
1 teaspoon mustard seeds

In a large mixing bowl, combine the cucumber slices, onion, bell pepper, and salt and mix well. Pack the mixture into 1-quart mason jars. In a medium saucepan over medium-high heat, combine the vinegar, sugar, celery seeds, and mustard seeds, bring to a boil, and cook until the sugar is dissolved. Remove from the heat and allow to cool for 1 hour, then pour the liquid over the cucumber mixture in the jars and seal tightly. Let the jars cool to room temperature, then refrigerate until ready to use. They'll keep for up to 1 week. If you're a canner, you can process the jars according to your canning equipment manufacturer's recommendations for other pickles.

FRIED GREEN TOMATOES

Serves 4 to 6 as an appetizer

Green tomatoes have always been a southern delicacy and have graced many a summer table. The bitterness cooks out and leaves a wonderful flavor when combined with the texture of the breading.

1 cup buttermilk

1 cup self-rising white cornmeal

¼ cup self-rising flour

1 teaspoon salt

½ teaspoon freshly ground black pepper

2 to 3 medium green tomatoes, thinly sliced, end slices discarded

½ cup canola oil

Red Pepper Mayo (page 116) or Juke Sauce (page 87), for serving

Fill a shallow bowl with the buttermilk. In a separate shallow bowl, hand-toss the cornmeal, flour, salt, and pepper. Place each tomato slice first in the bowl with the buttermilk and turn to coat well. Then transfer the slice to the breading mix, pressing it gently to cover. Flip it to coat both sides. Set aside the breaded slices on a plate.

Heat the oil in a small skillet over medium heat. Place several breaded slices in the skillet and cook for 2 minutes, then flip and cook for 1 minute longer or until crisp. Transfer to a paper-towel-lined plate to drain. Serve with Red Pepper Mayo or Juke Sauce.

PRALINE SWEET POTATO CASSEROLE

Serves 4 to 6

Sweet potatoes in Mississippi are kind of like shrimp to Forrest Gump. We have them fried, baked, mashed, or in pies—just about anything you can think of to do to a sweet potato, Mississippi folks have done. This dish is the standard, however, and it graces every holiday table in some form or fashion.

SWEET POTATO MIXTURE

4 pounds sweet potatoes

¾ cup whole milk

8 tablespoons (1 stick) unsalted butter

3 large eggs, lightly beaten

¾ cup packed dark brown sugar

PRALINE TOPPING

4 tablespoons (½ stick) unsalted butter

¾ cup packed dark brown sugar

½ teaspoon salt

½ teaspoon ground cinnamon

¾ cup heavy cream

1 cup chopped pecans

2 teaspoons vanilla extract

Preheat the oven to 350°F and grease a 9 by 13-inch baking dish. Boil the sweet potatoes until tender, drain, peel, and place in a large mixing bowl.

Heat the milk and butter in a small saucepan until simmering. Mash the potatoes and add the milk mixture, eggs, and brown sugar and blend well. Pour the mixture into the prepared pan.

To make the praline topping, melt the butter in a small saucepan over low medium-low heat, then stir in the brown sugar, salt, cinnamon, cream, and pecans. Bring to a simmer, but not a boil, and hold at that temperature for 5 to 6 minutes, stirring constantly. Remove from the heat and stir in the vanilla.

Pour the topping over the potatoes and bake for 30 minutes or until the topping reduces and gets a light crust.

CAST-IRON CORN BREAD

Serves 4 to 6

Many a meal has come out of my treasured cast-iron skillets. They are indispensable at my house. You can fry in them, make a roux, cook sausage or bacon, use them to roast, or, my favorite, bake corn bread. This is a simple, hearty bread that speaks to me about being raised in the country.

4 cups self-rising white cornmeal
1 cup self-rising flour
1 large egg
3 cups buttermilk
1 cup hot water

Preheat the oven to 450°F. Grease a 12-inch seasoned cast-iron skillet and place it in the oven to heat. Mix all the ingredients in a large mixing bowl, then carefully pour into the hot skillet. Bake for 20 to 25 minutes or until the crust is golden brown and the bread is firm. Remove from the oven and run a knife around the edges of the pan. Pry up and flip over the corn bread to keep the crust crisp. Serve hot.

GRILLED CORN IN THE HUSK

Serves 4

When I was young, my grandparents always grew corn in their garden and repeatedly warned me not to eat any. However, I would sneak out and nibble on the baby ears right off the stalk. Fast-forward to 2011, when I appeared on *Chopped* and one of the ingredients was baby corn ears. Ted Allen asked me if I had experience with baby corn, and I blurted out, "That's the first thing I ever stole!" Thank goodness that line didn't make the show! These days I don't have to steal my corn, and I like to cook it on the grill. Leaving the corn in the husk keeps it moister but allows some of the grill flavor to get to the corn.

4 ears sweet corn in the husk

2 tablespoons unsalted butter, melted

1 tablespoon finely chopped fresh cilantro

juice of 1 lime

2 tablespoons Fajita Seasoning (page 16)

Pull back the corn husk slightly and remove the silk. Replace the husk and soak the corn in cold water for 20 minutes. This will help steam the corn as it cooks.

Prepare a medium-hot grill. In a small bowl, mix the butter, cilantro, and lime juice. Remove the corn from the water and shake off excess. Pull the husks back (don't remove), brush the corn with the butter mixture, and season lightly with the fajita seasoning. Fold the husks back over the corn.

Place the corn on the grill and cook for about 10 minutes, turning occasionally. As the husk burns away, you will be able to see the outline of the kernels. That is a sign that that side is done. Remove the corn, remove the husks, and enjoy!

DEVILED EGGS

Makes 16

Most churches in the South have sign-up sheets for their potluck dinners. Otherwise, two out of three dishes would be deviled eggs. They're that popular around these parts. They also happen to be one of my favorite things in the world.

8 large eggs, hard-boiled and peeled

⅓ cup mayonnaise

2 tablespoons sweet pickle relish

½ teaspoon salt

½ teaspoon finely ground black pepper

1 teaspoon Ultimate BBQ Rub (page 14), in a shaker with fine holes

Cut the eggs in half lengthwise. Carefully remove the yolks and place them in a small bowl. Mash the yolks and stir in half of the mayonnaise and all of the pickle relish. Add additional mayonnaise 1 tablespoon at a time until your desired consistency is reached. Stir in the salt and pepper, then taste and adjust the seasonings. Fill the whites with the yolk mixture, then lightly sprinkle the tops with rub. Chill for at least 30 minutes before serving.

FIELD PEAS

Serves 4 to 6

Many of the foods we hated as a child are what we crave as an adult. For me, peas definitely fit the bill. I remember being forced to sit down and shell peas for hours and then being made to eat them—the horror! Nowadays, I'm first in line at any farmers' market when peas are in season. This recipe works for crowder peas, black-eyed peas, or purple-hull peas (which will leave their trademark color stained on your fingers for days, by the way). Adjust the cooking time as needed, though, as some will cook a little faster than others. Peas are best cooked simply, allowing their natural flavor to shine through.

4 cups freshly shelled peas
2½ cups water
About 2 tablespoons trimmings
from Makin' Bacon (page 66) or
your favorite brand or salt pork
1 teaspoon salt

Wash the peas and place them in a medium saucepan with the water, bacon, and salt. Bring to a boil over medium heat. Skim off any foam. Decrease the heat to low and simmer for 15 to 20 minutes or until the peas have the appropriate texture—not firm but not mushy. Taste and adjust the seasoning before serving.

One of the things I wanted to do when I opened Memphis Barbecue Company was to have desserts that were a cut above your average barbecue joint's offering of a slice of pie (though don't get me wrong—I love pie!). Our desserts are homemade and heartfelt, and I'm awfully proud to serve them. Some of these recipes were handed down to me, and some I've come up with by experimentation (usually with many not-so-good attempts, but that's a story for another day). I hope you enjoy them as much as I enjoy cooking them.

9
DESSERTS AND TREATS

MEYER LEMON PIE WITH WHIPPED CREAM

Makes 1 (9-inch) pie

I really like Meyer lemons, as they have a more subtle flavor than regular lemons. I keep the ingredients around to make this pie at all times, and when Meyers aren't in season, you can substitute regular lemons or even lemon juice in a pinch. It works great with key limes as well.

1½ cups graham cracker crumbs

⅓ cup granulated sugar

6 tablespoons (¾ stick) unsalted butter, melted

1 (14-ounce) can sweetened condensed milk

¾ cup freshly squeezed Meyer lemon juice

3 large egg yolks

Grated zest of 1 lemon

WHIPPED CREAM

1 cup heavy cream

1 tablespoon confectioners' sugar

½ teaspoon vanilla extract

Preheat the oven to 375°F. Mix the graham cracker crumbs, sugar, and butter and press into a 9-inch pie pan. Bake for 7 minutes and then cool completely. Reduce the oven temperature to 350°F.

In a medium mixing bowl, combine the sweetened condensed milk, lemon juice, egg yolks, and zest and mix on medium speed until smooth and slightly whipped, about 2 minutes. Pour into the pie shell and bake for 15 minutes, then remove and allow to cool.

Place the heavy cream in a medium mixing bowl and begin mixing on medium speed. As the cream starts to thicken, slowly add the confectioners' sugar and vanilla. Continue to beat and increase the speed to medium-high, until the whipped cream forms stiff peaks, about 2 minutes total. Spread the whipped cream over the pie before cutting or serve as a dollop on top of each slice.

TIP

Heavy cream is like buttermilk—it has a very long shelf life. I always keep some in the fridge for those unexpected visits!

OLD-FASHIONED BANANA PUDDING

Serves 4 to 6

Banana pudding is a cool, refreshing treat for a summer barbecue, and it is ubiquitous at southern gatherings. It's simple and yet so satisfying to enjoy a nice bowl after a grilled burger or smoked ribs.

1 cup sugar

½ cup all-purpose flour

1 teaspoon salt

4 large egg yolks

2 cups whole milk

1 teaspoon vanilla extract

1 tablespoon unsalted butter

1 (11-ounce) box vanilla wafers

5 medium bananas, sliced into
   ¼-inch rounds

Combine the sugar, flour, and salt in a mixing bowl and set aside. Beat the egg yolks well, then place them in a small saucepan over medium heat and whisk in the flour mixture. While whisking, slowly pour in the milk and vanilla. Bring to a boil, whisking constantly. As you see the mixture thicken, add the butter. Continue to whisk until the mixture becomes thick. Remove from the heat.

Line the bottom of a 9-inch square pan with vanilla wafers, then add a layer of sliced bananas. Pour approximately half of the pudding over the top, then make another layer of wafers and another banana layer, followed by the remaining pudding. Chill for at least 1 hour before serving.

GRILLED PINEAPPLE UPSIDE-DOWN CAKE

Serves 6 to 8

Don't be afraid to try different things on the grill. This brings in a little char and smoke and also uses my favorite pan, a cast-iron skillet. It's really fun to cook and even better to eat!

TOPPING

6 fresh pineapple rings, peeled and cored

2 tablespoons unsalted butter, melted

½ cup packed light brown sugar

¼ cup heavy cream

½ teaspoon freshly ground cinnamon

CAKE

1 cup cake flour

1 teaspoon baking powder

¼ teaspoon baking soda

½ teaspoon kosher salt

⅔ cup buttermilk (see Note, page 162)

2 large eggs

1 teaspoon dark rum (optional)

½ teaspoon vanilla extract

8 tablespoons (1 stick) unsalted butter

¾ cup granulated sugar

Prepare a medium-hot grill with the coals to one side. Lightly brush the pineapple rings with some of the butter and grill them long enough to get grill marks, 3 to 4 minutes. Remove and set aside.

In a 12-inch cast-iron skillet, combine the brown sugar, cream, cinnamon, and remaining butter and cook until the sugar dissolves and is bubbly. Remove the skillet from the heat and lay the pineapple rings across the bottom (cutting them in half if necessary to make them fit).

(Continued on page 162)

In a large bowl, mix together the flour, baking powder, baking soda, and salt. In a separate bowl, mix the buttermilk, eggs, rum, and vanilla. With an electric mixer on medium speed, cream the butter and granulated sugar until lightened, then pour in the buttermilk mixture and blend until smooth. Add in the flour mixture and blend for 1 minute, or until incorporated. Pour and spread the batter over the pineapples. Place the cake in the grill over indirect heat and cook for 45 minutes, maintaining the grill temperature around 350°F as closely as possible and keeping the cover closed. Check the cake by inserting a toothpick in the center. It should come out clean, and the top should be golden. Remove the cake from the grill and let rest for 5 minutes, then run a knife around the edges to loosen the cake. Put a large plate on top of the skillet and flip over, then slowly remove the skillet. Cool completely, then slice and serve.

NOTE

I like to use Bulgarian-style buttermilk if available. Bulgarian-style buttermilk is thicker and tangier than regular buttermilk, almost like Greek-style yogurt is to regular yogurt. It may be available in your local supermarket, but if not, just use regular buttermilk.

MOLASSES CANDY

Makes about 20 pieces

My grandmother Tracy would gracefully make this on occasion, and it was always a treat. Just be careful, as it could snatch a crown right off your tooth! Lard was traditionally used instead of shortening, and you could do the same.

1 tablespoon solid vegetable shortening

1 pound green (fresh) peanuts

1 teaspoon salt

¾ cup molasses, or more as needed

Heavily butter a 9 by 13-inch baking dish and have it ready. Also set aside a glass of very cold water (with no ice in it).

Melt the shortening in a saucepan over medium-low heat, add the peanuts and salt, and cook, stirring often, until the peanuts are hot and cooked, 5 to 7 minutes. Pour in the molasses, making sure it covers the peanuts and adding more if necessary. Continue to cook on medium-low until bubbly and the molasses lightens in color, about 5 minutes. Using a spoon, dip out a little of the molasses and drop it into the cold water. The mixture is done if it beads in the bottom of the glass and has a hard candy strand trailing down to it.

Pour the mixture into the buttered baking dish and allow to cool completely. Cut into serving sizes and enjoy.

MISSISSIPPI MUD PIE

Makes 1 (9-inch) pie

I've seen about 200 different Mississippi mud pie recipes, but they basically revolve around a brownie or chocolate cake with a marshmallow-type topping. This is one of my favorites of the bunch, and it makes for a deeply rich and decadent dessert. Use real vanilla extract, not the imitation kind.

FROSTING

6 tablespoons (¾ stick) unsalted butter

¼ cup plus 2 tablespoons unsweetened cocoa powder

2¾ cups confectioners' sugar, or more as needed

¼ cup plus 1 tablespoon evaporated milk, or more as needed

1 teaspoon vanilla extract

PIE

8 tablespoons (1 stick) unsalted butter, melted

2 large eggs, lightly beaten

2 teaspoons vanilla extract

¾ cup cake flour

1 cup granulated sugar

⅓ cup unsweetened cocoa powder

1 teaspoon baking powder

½ teaspoon salt

½ cup pecans, chopped and toasted lightly

1 cup mini marshmallows

Make the frosting: With a mixer on medium speed, cream the butter until smooth. In a separate bowl, mix together the cocoa and sugar, then lower the mixer speed and add the cocoa mixture to the butter mixture approximately 2 tablespoons at a time, alternating with 2 tablespoons of the evaporated milk. Continue to blend over low-medium until all the cocoa and milk is blended. Add the vanilla and continue to blend, increasing the speed to medium, until the frosting is light and fluffy. Taste and add more confectioners' sugar or evaporated milk if necessary to adjust the flavor and consistency. Set aside.

Preheat the oven to 350°F. Butter a 9-inch springform pan. In a mixing bowl, with a mixer on low speed, blend the butter, eggs, and vanilla. Add the flour, granulated sugar, cocoa, baking powder, and salt and mix for 1 minute. Stir in the pecans with a spatula, then pour the batter into the prepared pan. Bake for 25 minutes, then check the center with a toothpick. It should come out clean. The baking may take up to 30 minutes, but try not to overcook. Spread the marshmallows over the top and return to the oven for 3 to 4 minutes or until the marshmallows are soft. Remove from the oven and spread the chocolate frosting over the top. Allow to cool until set.

BLACKBERRY CRÈME BRÛLÉE

Serves 6

Crème brûlée is way easier than it looks. This is a simple yet impressive dessert you can make in advance and "burn" right before you serve. You do need a torch, available at any hardware store or most culinary stores. I use 8-ounce ramekins for this dish, though traditionally smaller, shallower ramekins are used. I modeled this after fruit-on-the-bottom yogurt. A lot of crème brûlées are served with a topping sauce or have a flavoring mixed in, but I had never seen it layered. I like it because you get the creaminess of the custard and still get the full flavor of the blackberries.

BLACKBERRY REDUCTION

2 pints fresh or frozen
   blackberries (see Notes)
¼ cup water
¾ cup granulated sugar
1½ teaspoons cornstarch
1½ teaspoons water

CUSTARD

4 cups heavy cream
1 vanilla bean, split and scraped
½ cup granulated sugar
6 large egg yolks
2 tablespoons turbinado sugar
   (see Notes)

Whipped cream (page 158) for
   serving
Fresh mint leaves for garnish

Place the berries and water in a heavy saucepan and cook for 20 minutes, mashing as you stir. Add the ¾ cup of granulated sugar, bring to a boil, then decrease the heat and simmer until reduced by half, about 15 minutes. In a small bowl, stir together the cornstarch and water to form a slurry. Add the slurry to the berry mixture, bring to a boil, then decrease the heat and simmer for 4 to 5 minutes. Remove from the heat and allow to cool to room temperature.

Place the cream and vanilla bean and seeds in a medium saucepan and bring to a boil. Remove from the heat and allow to cool for 15 to 20 minutes. Remove the vanilla pod. In a medium mixing bowl, whisk together the ½ cup of granulated sugar and the egg yolks until well blended. Temper the eggs by adding the hot cream mixture a little at a time while whisking. Continue until you have whisked in all the cream mixture.

Preheat the oven to 325°F. Spoon about 1½ tablespoons of the blackberry mixture into the bottom of each of 6 (8-ounce) ramekins. (Reserve the extra sauce from the reduction for garnishing the desserts.) Top each with custard to within ⅓ inch of the top of the ramekin and place in a 2-inch-deep pan large enough to contain all of the ramekins. Pour hot water into the pan to halfway up the sides of the ramekins. Carefully transfer the pan to the oven and bake for 40 to 45 minutes, until the custards are set with just a small jiggle in the middle. Remove from the oven, remove the ramekins from the pan, and allow to cool for at least 3 hours. At this point, you can wrap each ramekin and refrigerate for up to 2 days before serving.

Just before serving, sprinkle approximately 1 teaspoon of the turbinado sugar evenly over the top of each custard. Follow your torch manufacturer's operation instructions and gently torch the sugar on top of each custard until caramelized and fragrant. Garnish each custard with whipped cream and a mint leaf, place on a serving plate, and drizzle a teaspoon of blackberry syrup on each plate.

NOTES

I grew up on blackberries and don't mind the seeds. If you would like to remove them, press the mixture while hot through a chinois or fine-mesh sieve.

Granulated sugar is traditional, but it burns quite easily when torched. Turbinado gives a nice golden crust with a hint of molasses flavor.

BREAD PUDDING WITH CARAMEL SAUCE

Serves 6 to 8

We've been making bread pudding out of doughnuts for years at home and at the restaurants. The most important component is a nice light yeast donut. Never use cake style. We started this recipe using Shipley's donuts from near my hometown in Greenville, Mississippi, many years ago, and as many different doughnuts as I've tried, they are still the best for the recipe—airy and light and not too sweet. Luckily, there is a Shipley's just a half mile from our restaurant in Horn Lake, Mississippi, so we still use them today, but your local independent doughnut shop would be just fine too.

2 dozen yeast doughnuts, torn
   into ½-inch pieces
1 (14-ounce) can sweetened
   condensed milk
½ (20-ounce) can apple pie filling
2 large eggs, lightly beaten
1 teaspoon kosher salt
¾ cup heavy cream

CARAMEL SAUCE

1 pound (4 sticks) unsalted
   butter
2 cups packed light brown sugar
⅓ cup heavy cream

Preheat the oven to 350°F.

Place the doughnut pieces in a large mixing bowl and add the condensed milk, apple pie filling, eggs, salt, and the ¾ cup of cream. Mix thoroughly, then press down on the mixture to form a flat surface. Allow to sit for 20 minutes to let the doughnuts absorb the moisture, then place in a 9 by 13-inch pan and press down to distribute evenly. The pudding should be around 1½ inches thick. Bake for 45 minutes or until golden brown on top.

To make the caramel sauce, melt the butter in a small saucepan over medium heat and add the brown sugar. Continue cooking and bring to a very slight boil, stirring often, until the sugar is fully dissolved. You can taste it to see if the graininess is gone. Add the ⅓ cup of cream and whisk to incorporate.

Spoon the bread pudding into bowls and top with the warm caramel sauce.

SWEET POTATO PIE

Makes 1 (9-inch) pie

I will readily admit that I am not a good cook of that most traditional of southern pies, the pecan pie. It just doesn't work right for me. However, my sweet potato pie is pretty dang good. The meringue recipe makes enough for a modest topping. If you want a big, soaring meringue on your pie, double or even triple the recipe.

2 large sweet potatoes, boiled
4 tablespoons (½ stick) unsalted
    butter, melted
1 cup sugar
2 large eggs
¼ teaspoon salt
½ teaspoon ground cinnamon
½ teaspoon freshly grated
    nutmeg
¼ teaspoon ground cloves
1 cup evaporated milk
1 (9-inch) unbaked pie shell

MERINGUE
1 teaspoon lemon juice
3 large egg whites
¼ teaspoon salt
¼ teaspoon vanilla extract
¼ cup plus 2 tablespoons sugar

Preheat the oven to 350°F. In a large mixing bowl, mash the sweet potatoes and stir in the butter, the 1 cup of sugar, eggs, salt, cinnamon, nutmeg, cloves, and evaporated milk. Pour the filling into the shell and bake for 35 minutes or until firm.

As the pie finishes baking, make the meringue. Place the lemon juice, egg whites, salt, and vanilla in a medium mixing bowl and beat on medium speed until the mixture starts to get foamy. Add the sugar in 1-tablespoon increments while beating until the sugar dissolves and the mixture forms stiff peaks.

Remove the pie from the oven, top with the meringue, and return to the oven for 15 minutes or until the meringue is golden brown.

PINTO BEAN PIE

Makes 1 (9-inch) pie

I first made this on a lark, and lo and behold, people liked it! If you didn't know any better, you would never guess it had pinto beans in it.

⅓ cup cooked pinto beans

6 tablespoons (¾ cup) unsalted butter, melted

1 large egg

1 teaspoon vanilla extract

1 cup granulated sugar

½ cup shredded sweetened coconut

⅓ cup chopped pecans

1 (9-inch) unbaked pie shell

Whipped cream (page 158) for serving

Preheat the oven to 300°F. Mash the beans. Add the butter, egg, vanilla, sugar, coconut, and pecans and stir for 2 minutes, until well mixed and slightly aerated. Pour the filling into the shell and bake for 1 hour. Allow to cool completely, then slice and serve with a dollop of whipped cream. Don't tell anyone you used pinto beans.

CAYENNE GRILLED PEACHES

Serves 4

I'm big on different flavors in the same dish. This has the sweetness of the brown sugar, the luxurious freshness of the peaches, and a little kick in the back from the cayenne.

4 peaches
3 tablespoons light brown sugar
1 teaspoon vanilla extract
1 teaspoon cayenne
Whipped cream (page 158) for serving

Prepare a hot grill.

Cut the peaches in half and remove the pits. In a small bowl, mix together the brown sugar, vanilla, and cayenne. Place the peach halves in a baking dish cut side up and spoon the sugar mixture over the peaches. Allow to sit for 20 minutes or until the sugar dissolves.

Place the peaches on the grill skin side down and cook for about 3 minutes or until they develop some char and the sugar is slightly set. Turn over and grill for 1 minute, then quarter turn them to develop a nice diamond-shaped grill mark. Remove, place on serving plates, and serve with a dollop of whipped cream.

ACKNOWLEDGMENTS

Delta cuisine is straightforward, but, for me at least, writing a cookbook is not. This work is a compilation of my memories growing up in the Delta, my career in the restaurant business, and my life on the competition barbecue circuit. As such, it was quite a task blending a lifetime of recipes into a coherent book—at least I certainly hope that's what I did. None of this would have been possible without some very important people in my life, and though I cannot thank everyone by name who has helped, I would like to express thanks to a few people who have been instrumental both in my life and in the creation of this book.

My grandfather, Quinton Pounders, was a shining example of what's good in America. A humble man, he served his country in the Pacific during horrific battles that he would never talk about—but you knew the memories haunted him for the remainder of his life. He taught me humility, hard work, pride, and personal responsibility. I'll always be grateful to have been his granddaughter. He was the most honest man I've ever known, and I hope that I've made him proud.

My husband, Pete, and I have been through the good times and the bad, but we've walked hand in hand no matter what.

My daughter, Lauren, doesn't realize how special she really is. I'm so proud to be her mother. Lauren, I know it hasn't always been easy to be my daughter, but you have become a beautiful lady and I hope that someday you'll understand that Mommy has done everything to make a better life for you (even if you decide you don't want to follow in my footsteps—which I wouldn't suggest, by the way).

My mother, Beverly Weaver, had faith that we could win, even when we didn't believe in ourselves.

Lane Butler and the team at Andrews McMeel Publishing believed in me, and my story. Thank you so much.

Thanks also to the many customers of Memphis Barbecue Company. Every single day when I wake up, I am thankful for you, as the great success of the restaurants has given me the opportunity to keep chasing my dreams and rewarded me with knowing that people like our cooking. Thank you!

METRIC CONVERSIONS AND EQUIVALENTS

METRIC CONVERSION FORMULAS

To Convert	Multiply
Ounces to grams	Ounces by 28.35
Pounds to kilograms	Pounds by 0.454
Teaspoons to milliliters	Teaspoons by 4.93
Tablespoons to milliliters	Tablespoons by 14.79
Fluid ounces to milliliters	Fluid ounces by 29.57
Cups to milliliters	Cups by 236.59
Cups to liters	Cups by 0.236
Pints to liters	Pints by 0.473
Quarts to liters	Quarts by 0.946
Gallons to liters	Gallons by 3.785
Inches to centimeters	Inches by 2.54

Common Ingredients and THEIR APPROXIMATE EQUIVALENTS

1 cup uncooked rice = 225 grams
1 cup all-purpose flour = 140 grams
1 stick butter (4 ounces • ½ cup • 8 tablespoons) = 110 grams
1 cup butter (8 ounces • 2 sticks • 16 tablespoons) = 220 grams
1 cup brown sugar, firmly packed = 225 grams
1 cup granulated sugar = 200 grams

APPROXIMATE METRIC EQUIVALENTS

Volume

¼ teaspoon	1 milliliter
½ teaspoon	2.5 milliliters
¾ teaspoon	4 milliliters
1 teaspoon	5 milliliters
1¼ teaspoons	6 milliliters
1½ teaspoons	7.5 milliliters
1¾ teaspoons	8.5 milliliters
2 teaspoons	10 milliliters
1 tablespoon (½ fluid ounce)	15 milliliters
2 tablespoons (1 fluid ounce)	30 milliliters
¼ cup	60 milliliters
⅓ cup	80 milliliters
½ cup (4 fluid ounces)	120 milliliters
⅔ cup	160 milliliters
¾ cup	180 milliliters
1 cup (8 fluid ounces)	240 milliliters
1¼ cups	300 milliliters
1½ cups (12 fluid ounces)	360 milliliters
1⅔ cups	400 milliliters
2 cups (1 pint)	460 milliliters
3 cups	700 milliliters
4 cups (1 quart)	0.95 liter
1 quart plus ¼ cup	1 liter
4 quarts (1 gallon)	3.8 liters

Weight

¼ ounce	7 grams
½ ounce	14 grams
¾ ounce	21 grams
1 ounce	28 grams
1¼ ounces	35 grams
1½ ounces	42.5 grams
1⅔ ounces	45 grams
2 ounces	57 grams
3 ounces	85 grams
4 ounces (¼ pound)	113 grams
5 ounces	142 grams
6 ounces	170 grams
7 ounces	198 grams
8 ounces (½ pound)	227 grams
16 ounces (1 pound)	454 grams
35.25 ounces (2.2 pounds)	1 kilogram

Length

⅛ inch	3 millimeters
¼ inch	6 millimeters
½ inch	1.25 centimeters
1 inch	2.5 centimeters
2 inches	5 centimeters
2½ inches	6 centimeters
4 inches	10 centimeters
5 inches	13 centimeters
6 inches	15.25 centimeters
12 inches (1 foot)	30 centimeters

OVEN TEMPERATURES

To convert Fahrenheit to Celsius, subtract 32 from Fahrenheit, multiply the result by 5, then divide by 9.

Description	Fahrenheit	Celsius	British Gas Mark
Very cool	200°	95°	0
Very cool	225°	110°	¼
Very cool	250°	120°	½
Cool	275°	135°	1
Cool	300°	150°	2
Warm	325°	165°	3
Moderate	350°	175°	4
Moderately hot	375°	190°	5
Fairly hot	400°	200°	6
Hot	425°	220°	7
Very hot	450°	230°	8
Very hot	475°	245°	9

Information compiled from a variety of sources, including *Recipes into Type* by Joan Whitman and Dolores Simon (Newton, MA: Biscuit Books, 2000); *The New Food Lover's Companion* by Sharon Tyler Herbst (Hauppauge, NY: Barron's, 1995); and *Rosemary Brown's Big Kitchen Instruction Book* (Kansas City, MO: Andrews McMeel, 1998).

INDEX